What Experts Are Saying about
The Great American Supper Swap

I love The Great American Supper Swap *because it helps families once again gather around the table for dinner—with less stress. Chockfull of practical advice, real-life stories, and huge helpings of encouragement, this book serves as a valuable addition to a mom's hectic life.*

—MARY E. DEMUTH, AUTHOR OF *ORDINARY MOM, EXTRAORDINARY GOD;* AND
BUILDING THE CHRISTIAN FAMILY YOU NEVER HAD

Trish's book comes at a crucial time in the shaping of the next generation of America. Today's moms are frazzled and overwhelmed with our family's schedules, and eating an evening meal together at home is often the first thing to go. Trish's ideas will revolutionize the way today's families connect and share meals together.

—HEATHER IVESTER, AUTHOR OF *FROM A DAUGHTER'S HEART TO HER MOM*

Author Trish Berg unites faith, food, and family in The Great American Supper Swap, *which is an enjoyable, easy-to-read story of how families support each other in so much more than sharing food.*

—CARON GOODE, ED.D., FOUNDER OF ACADEMY FOR COACHING PARENTS, LLC,
AND AUTHOR OF *HELP KIDS COPE WITH STRESS & TRAUMA*

The
Great
American
Supper
Swap

Trish Berg

The Great American Supper Swap

Solving the Busy Woman's
Family Dinnertime
Dilemma

LIFE JOURNEY®
Bringing Home the Message for Life

COOK COMMUNICATIONS MINISTRIES
Colorado Springs, Colorado • Paris, Ontario
KINGSWAY COMMUNICATIONS LTD
Eastbourne, England

Life Journey® is an imprint of
Cook Communications Ministries, Colorado Springs, CO 80918
Cook Communications, Paris, Ontario
Kingsway Communications, Eastbourne, England

THE GREAT AMERICAN SUPPER SWAP
© 2007 by Trish Berg

Published in association with the literary agency of Les Stobbe, 300 Doubleday Road, Tryon, NC, 28782.

The Web addresses (URLs) recommended throughout this book are solely offered as a resource to the reader. The citation of these Web sites does not in any way imply an endorsement on the part of the author or the publisher, nor does the author or publisher vouch for their content for the life of this book.

Photos: Corbis, Photos.com, istockphoto.com
Cover Design: Koechel Peterson & Associates
Interior Design: Karen Athen

First Printing, 2007
Printed in the United States of America

1 2 3 4 5 6 7 8 9 10

All Scripture quotations, unless otherwise noted, are taken from the *Holy Bible, New International Version*®. *NIV*®. Copyright © 1973, 1978, 1984 by International Bible Society. Used by permission of Zondervan. All rights reserved. Scripture quotations marked NLT are taken from the *Holy Bible, New Living Translation*, copyright © 1996. Used by permission of Tyndale House Publishers, Inc., Wheaton, Illinois 60189. All rights reserved; and KJV are taken from the King James Version of the Bible. (Public Domain.)

The brand names mentioned in this book are not endorsed by the author or the publisher, nor do we guarantee the results of using those brands.

ISBN 978-0-7814-4388-3
LCCN 2006932569

Contents

Part One

WHAT'S FOR DINNER?

Part Two

YOU NEED MORE CHEFS IN YOUR KITCHEN

Forever and always,
to the love of my life, best friend,
biggest fan, and devoted husband, Michael

Acknowledgments

My Supper-Swapping Girlfriends: Heartfelt hugs to my supper-swapping girlfriends: Carla, Amy, Audrey, Teri, Nann, and Kelly. I enjoy swapping so much more than meals with you and hold you dearly in my heart. And thanks to Annie Weaver for starting the trend!

My Writing Friends: Thanks to my mentor, Beth Jusino. I doubt I would be where I am without your encouragement. Thanks to Brenda Nixon, Cathy Messecar, Karen Robbins, Leslie Wilson, Terra Hangen, Lori Scott, and Heather Ivester for supporting and inspiring me, praying for me, and reminding me that I am always a wife and a mom first.

My Team: Thanks to everyone who read, edited, encouraged, and prayed for this book—especially Mike, Don and Kay, Mary Ann and Jerry, Diane, Carla, Teri, Kelly and Dave, Nann and Mark, Barb and Mark, Gail, Lisa, Erin, and all the MOPS moms and women's groups I have been blessed to speak to. Thanks to my column editors at *The Daily Record*: Lance White, Lydia Gehring, Ann Gasbarre, for giving me a platform to speak to readers. To all my column fans in Ohio, thanks for your constant encouragement. And my heartfelt appreciation to Kelli Standish and Pulsepoint Web Design for connecting me to the world.

Les Stobbe: Thanks for believing in my writing, blessing my life, and guiding my career.

Mike Nappa: Thanks for taking a chance on a new author.

Cook Communications: Thank you to Lora Schrock, Diane Gardner, and all the wonderful editors and staff for sharing my vision for this book and for ministering to moms everywhere.

My Family: Thank you, Mike, for prioritizing our family and our faith. Thanks also go to my children—Hannah, Sydney, Colin, and Riley—for teaching me how important our family suppers are. To my parents—Mom and Dad Pearson and Mom and Dad Berg—for loving my family and giving us roots. To my sisters and brothers by birth and marriage—for surrounding our family with cousins and love. To my St. Michaels and Camp Luther family— for faithfully proclaiming the gospel and leading me to Christ. And to Ma Ma Hart—for teaching me that family and faith go hand in hand.

My Savior: Most of all, I praise the Lord for blessing me beyond my wildest dreams, and I pray that these words are his words, and that they bless your family.

Foreword

Family is so very important to me. Other than my salvation, it is the most precious gift God has given me. In our home, we created many family memories when our well-known son, Michael, and his sister, Kimberly, were growing up. Now we're enjoying many more with their families and our grandchildren—and even great-grandchildren.

Many life experiences are shared in our homes around the table; it's a place of bonding together where we feel loved, comfortable, and accepted. It's a place where we express thankfulness to our heavenly Father for everything he has given us as we share a meal with loved ones and friends. And it's a place where we discover the pleasure of extending mealtime beyond physical nourishment to something more. It is our mission as moms not only to feed the body but also to nurture the soul.

But most moms I know are over-worked and under-rested. It seems there is so little time that we have to constantly multitask our days. So how do we accomplish all that is required of us? By seeking God's wisdom and guidance daily and asking him to orchestrate our days. And he always supplies an abundance of wisdom through special people and unique tools he chooses to place in our lives.

Trish Berg has discovered one of these special tools—and shares it with the rest of us within the pages of *The Great American Supper Swap*.

What a great concept—sharing meals and building relationships while gaining time! But this book encompasses so much
more: growing friendships, meal simplification, budgeting basics,
nutrition guidelines, time management, and God's Word. And the
rewards of swapping suppers are more time, less stress, and opening our hearts to those with whom we share these meals. It has
been said that for every person you meet you add a chapter to
your life. Supper swapping adds volumes. What a blessing!

I pray that God will richly bless you and yours as you use this
book to reap the rewards offered herein.

—BARBARA SMITH,
AUTHOR OF *FOOD THAT SAYS WELCOME*,
MOTHER TO SINGER/SONGWRITER MICHAEL W. SMITH

Introduction

The Dinnertime Blues

Every afternoon the *"What's for dinner?"* question crept into my thoughts, dragging me down and stealing my positive attitude. Mothering my kids seemed to be all I could manage most days. Well, that and—on a good day—maybe a few loads of laundry.

And let's face it: I'm not a chef. Although I love to eat, I don't love to cook. So where did that leave me? Usually serving quick-fix meals, cold cereal, grilled-cheese sandwiches, or ordering pizza.

That was until five years ago when supper swapping came into my life.

Supper swapping is moms helping moms by sharing the cooking responsibilities for their families. One day a week you cook enough food for everyone in your group, usually three to five families. You keep one meal for your family and deliver the other meals to the families in your group. The rest of the week, they deliver supper to you. It's like hiring a caterer for free!

Supper swapping maximizes the impact of your labor. It's much simpler to shop for the ingredients and then prepare five identical meals than it is to shop for and prepare five completely different meals. For one to two hours of meal preparation and thirty minutes of meal-delivery time once a week, you have an entire week's worth of homemade meals for your family to enjoy.

The Popularity of Supper Swapping

Supper swapping is catching on in rural areas and big cities alike, with stay-at-home moms and working moms, big families and small ones. It's not surprising that people are searching for a better way to do dinner. With today's simultaneous trends of increasingly busy families and refocusing on the importance of community, supper swapping has become a growing grassroots phenomenon spreading rapidly from coast to coast.

Feature articles on supper swapping have appeared in *Today's Christian Woman* (September/October 2006), *Better Homes and Gardens* (March 2005), *Quick Cooking* (February 2005), *Working Mother* (May 2004), *Southern Living* (August 2003), and MOPS International's *MOMSense* magazine (March 2004). Why is it catching on so fast? Because it's simple—and it simply works!

Supper Swapping Is Life Sharing

But supper swapping is more than just meal sharing—it's *life* sharing. God calls us to love one another, and supper swapping is a wonderful opportunity to do just that. "A new command I give you: Love one another. As I have loved you, so you must love one another" (John 13:34). Love is not passive or stagnant. Love is an action, a decision we make each day. We choose to love others in what we say *and* in what we do. Supper swapping is one way we can show our love by cooking for each other and helping nourish our families with so much more than food.

Beyond your front porch. Supper swapping also provides moms with an incredible opportunity for relational evangelism. It opens the door to building stronger friendships and witnessing to neighbors and friends in two ways. First, by forming supper-swapping groups, moms are able to build strong friendships around the commonalities of motherhood and cooking, showing their love and sharing their faith. Second, by preparing an extra meal on their cooking day and sharing it with a family in need outside of their supper-swapping group, moms can witness to neighbors and friends, giving as Christ calls us to give.

Let me give you an example. I know how stressful and exhausting it is being married to a coach. My husband, Mike, is a high school math teacher and baseball coach. Every spring, life is hectic at our house.

Kathy's husband also coaches at a nearby high school. When his team was in the state football playoffs last year, I knew life would be busy for her. So instead of making four Cheesy Chicken Pot Pies that week, I made five and delivered the extra one to Kathy. With little added expense or effort, I was able to serve supper to another family, reaching beyond my own front porch.

Joining a family of families. I grew up in a very small family—just my mom, dad, sister, and me. Then I married Mike and suddenly was a member of this huge extended family about the size of Montana. It was a bit overwhelming at first, but I've found my place in this clan and have discovered the blessings of a big family.

Family is an important part of who we are. Big or small, our family defines, influences, and loves us. I've surrounded myself with loving, caring people—some related by blood and others bound by friendship. They're all important to me. They're all family. And through supper swapping, I've added to my circle of love and built an even bigger family.

Who is there to help or to celebrate your joys or to cry at your sorrows? Family. You don't have to be born into the perfect family. What you do need to do is appreciate your family for who they are and extend that family through added friendships. Reach out to others and watch God reach out to you through them.

Fellowship and family are very important to God. He cares about both our physical nourishment and our soul's need for community:

- God provided manna from heaven to feed his children in the desert (see Ex. 16:4 and John 6:31).
- Jesus' first miracle was to turn water into wine at a wedding (see John 2:1–11).
- Jesus took the humble offering of a simple boy—five loaves of bread and two fish—and fed five thousand (see Matt. 14:13–21).

Whether your family is big or small, God wants you to join with other families. Get to know your neighbors. Join a church. Fellowship with others. Nourish your hunger for him by loving one another. Supper swapping is a wonderful way to reflect God's desire for our fellowship and nourishment.

Supper versus Dinner

I grew up in northern Ohio eating lunch at noon and dinner in the evening. Then Mike and I married and moved one hour south to the farming town where he was raised. Suddenly, I was eating dinner at noon and supper in the evening. It can be quite confusing. Many regional and familial traditions use the terms *dinner* and *supper* to mean different things.

The history of these words is interesting. The American colonists typically ate their largest meal midafternoon, calling it dinner. In the nineteenth century, families who lived in rural areas, whether farming or working blue-collar jobs, continued to eat their largest meal of the day at noon, also calling it dinner. They ate a simple meal in the evening and referred to that as supper.

In the twentieth century, however, urban families began referring to their evening meal as dinner, whether it was a simple meal or a four-course masterpiece. However, on Sundays or holidays, it was the noon meal that was referred to as dinner (i.e., Christmas dinner). So the distinction became more of a demographic and geographic one.

According to research conducted by Professor Bert Vaux from Harvard University, when asked, "What is the distinction between dinner and supper?" families said:

- Supper is an evening meal, while dinner is eaten earlier (lunch, for example) (7.79%).
- Supper is an evening meal; dinner is the main meal (7.76%).
- Dinner takes place in a more formal setting than supper (12.12%).
- There is no distinction; they both have the same meaning (34.56%).
- I do not use the term *supper* (33.14%).
- I do not use the term *dinner* (0.82%).
- Other (3.83%).

It's amazing that Mike and I grew up in the same state just one hour away from each other, and yet we used different terms describing our evening meal. So, for the sake of fairness, both terms will be used interchangeably in this book to describe the evening meal, whether it's simple fare or an extravagant delight.

A Family-Friendly Solution

Supper or dinner, the evening meal has always been an important ingredient in helping to build family communication, commitment, and unity. Families in America need to come back to the dinner table and give their kids a taste of love.

Supper swapping is a simple solution to your dinnertime dilemma that can open up many opportunities for you to exhibit godly love and service. It can also help to ensure that your priorities are God's priorities. (How this happens will be discussed later in the book.) *The Great American Supper Swap* was designed with you in mind. I've created short, easy-to-read sections so you can quickly find what you're looking for.

In chapter 15, you'll find inspirational Scriptures and sayings you can encourage each other with when you jot them down on your baking instructions at meal delivery. Chapter 16 will answer all of your supper-swapping questions in a Q&A format. Chapter 17 has great supper-swapping recipes to get you started. And finally, you'll find kid-friendly mealtime prayers, cooking conversion tables, and all the supper-swapping resources you'll need in the three appendixes.

Claim the magic for your family. I'll show you how. Don't give in. Don't give up. Just get swapping! What do you have to lose, except that familiar four-thirty-and-nothing's-in-the-oven panic? And what you're bound to gain is so much more than you can imagine!

Part One

WHAT'S FOR DINNER?

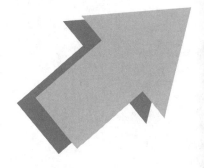

One

FOOD FOLLIES

Let Supper Swapping Simplify Your Life

Reality Motherhood

More than a decade ago, when we brought our first child, Hannah, home from the hospital, we were greeted by a parade of family and friends. They all wanted to hold our new baby girl, and they all began to tell me how to be a mom.

Everyone had advice, and I tried desperately to soak it all in. Sleep when the baby sleeps. Don't worry about the laundry. Only feed her every two hours. Feed her whenever she cries. Don't use a pacifier to calm

> *So do not worry, saying, "What shall we eat?" or "What shall we drink?" or "What shall we wear?" But seek first his kingdom and his righteousness, and all these things will be given to you as well.*
>
> MATTHEW 6:31, 33

her. Pacifiers are the best. Put her on your schedule; don't adapt to hers. Whew!

Like a whirlwind, the suggestions came in and swept my sanity away. Or maybe it was the lack of sleep that did that. Either way, I was a nervous wreck for most of that first year, trying to do everything right and usually doing most of it wrong.

Now I'm older, grayer, and hopefully a little wiser. I have four children to mother, ages eleven to four, and I have even more questions and concerns than I had back then. How do I handle back talk? When should I give them more freedom? When should I push potty training? When time-outs don't work, what's next?

There seem to be more questions than answers, more things to stress about than I ever could have imagined. Supper had become just something else I worried about and often got wrong. Life is full of enough stresses—supper shouldn't be one of them!

Before I began supper swapping, cooking for my family was just one more item on my daily to-do list, one more ball I had to keep in the air. But now, I have to prepare only one meal one night a week, and the rest of the week my to-do list is minimized by one less chore. We have four families in our supper-swapping group, so three days a week, I know that supper is being delivered, and I don't have to lift a finger. We also have enough leftovers for a fifth meal, covering the entire workweek.

Supper swapping won't solve all your stresses, but it *will* eliminate the stress you feel every day at 4:30 p.m. when nothing's in the oven. It will create a more relaxed home in the evenings, and you might even find the time to read a book here and there. It will simplify your grocery-shopping list and bless you with a group of moms to stand by your side.

Yesterday, I asked my friend Teri what she loved most about supper swapping. She told me, "Since I've been swapping suppers, I've made fewer trips to the grocery store because I shop with a plan. I spend less on groceries, less on gas, and best of all, I have more time each day for what's truly important—spending time with my kids."

Pirates and Picky Eaters

Do you ever feel as if you are at war? Well, you are. I have seen the enemy and it is four feet tall. Each one has a will of steel, a scream louder than an oncoming locomotive, and an earsplitting whine that sounds like a jet flying low overhead.

They can attack you at any moment, from any angle, taking

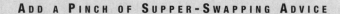

ADD A PINCH OF SUPPER-SWAPPING ADVICE

For your picky-eater pirates, put only a small amount of food on your children's plates, but require them to eat that amount. We use a tablespoon as our minimum must-try amount of everything we are having for supper.

Once supper is served, you can set your microwave timer for thirty or forty minutes. Your picky eaters must finish the minimum amount on their plate before the timer beeps or they face a consequence. They could lose their bedtime story or go to bed early. The key is to remove yourself from the battle. Don't yell. Don't get angry. Just follow through on the consequence. It really works!

Try to include one or two meals each week that most of the kids in your

you completely by surprise, especially at the dinner table. Like pirates at sea jumping on a ship to pillage it, they steal your strength and energy, your positive attitude, and your joyful mood. They are the picky-eater pirates, and they are on the attack.

I've fought many wars with my own picky-eater pirates over the battle of the broccoli and the skirmish of the squash. I've won some battles and lost some. I have battle scars to prove it. In my weaker moments, I've surrendered, waved the white flag (usually a tissue), and given in to their demands. I've let them eat peanut butter and jelly sandwiches or chicken nuggets for supper. Sometimes I do what works and survive to fight another day.

supper-swapping group will enjoy. Kid-friendly recipes like baked macaroni and cheese or spaghetti work well.

Ask for your preteens' or teenagers' input, and include meals they like and can help you prepare. Invite them to be part of the process.

Make a list of all the things you do throughout each day, and then rank and do them in order of importance. How does supper fit into your schedule now?

Have a family meeting and discuss the possibility of joining or forming a supper-swapping group.

List your family's ten favorite meals, and discuss any food dislikes they have. Remember everyone's food allergies too.

Pray about your family supper, and seek God's will. Don't leave God out of the decision process.

Mealtime should be peaceful, not a battle. But with kids, it's often a challenge. That's one reason I decided to start swapping suppers, and it has definitely helped me fight my picky-eater pirates. Now I have an army of moms to help me win at the dinner table. My kids still may turn their noses up at what is on their plates, but I'm not as emotionally tied to the meal, and I'm certainly not as exhausted at the end of the day.

My kids are even trying new foods. I guess it's the grass-is-always-greener syndrome. They enjoy eating the meals other moms in my swapping group prepare and deliver. All in all, our suppertime battles are fewer and farther between, and our family meals are much calmer.

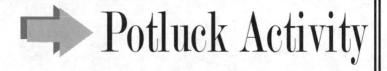 # Potluck Activity

MOMMY MUST-DOS

Here is a great get-to-know-you activity to share with your supper-swapping girlfriends at your next meal-planning gathering.

Give each person a sheet of paper and have her tear it into ten pieces. On each of the first five pieces of paper, write down one mommy must-do you dislike, from laundry to dishes, sweeping to diaper changing. Then, on each of the other five pieces of paper write one mommy must-do you enjoy, like reading bedtime stories or baking cookies. When you're all done, put them into a bowl. One at a time, draw each slip out and read it to the group. Try to guess whether it's a like or dislike and who wrote it. See who can guess the most right—and who actually enjoys scrubbing the toilet.

Dear Lord, we thank you for the blessing of family and friendship, for loved ones who surround us with warmth and comfort. Sometimes we get frazzled with our daily demands and stressful schedules. Help us to slow down and enjoy life, to seek your will for our families so we may find peace and joy once again around our dinner table. Lead us as we embark on supper swapping, and help us to simplify our suppers and share our faith with others. Amen.

Two

THE DISAPPEARING DINNER

The Deterioration of the Family Meal

What Is Dinner to a Child?

When I was a little girl, we frequently hung out at our dining-room table. We all played, colored pictures, and ate supper at the dining-room table. It was one of those old-fashioned, Formica-topped tables—shiny and smooth and slippery as a seal. Probably not something that will eventually become an antique, but treasured by us nonetheless.

> *When I consider your heavens, the work of your fingers, the moon and the stars, which you have set in place, what is man that you are mindful of him, the son of man that you care for him?*
>
> PSALM 8:3–4

We lived in a barn-red ranch home that sat back near the woods, far from the road. We had almost two acres of land around our house, room to roam, and woods to explore. We had a huge yard, and in the spring I would rush home from school as fast as my string-bean legs would carry me just so I could play back there before it got dark.

There was no rushing from soccer to piano lessons, gymnastics to swimming. We had time to kill when I was a kid, hours to fill using nothing but our imaginations. We played outside in the big backyard with all the neighborhood kids. We did a whole lot of nothing some days. When kickball or freeze tag sounded boring, we would make up a new game. Once it started getting dark, my mom would call us in for supper.

You know, as hard as I try, I can't remember a thing my mom made for supper. Not a single homemade meal stands out in my mind. My mom was a good cook, but what we ate wasn't as important as the fact that we ate it together. She gave me more than food. She gave me her time and attention. That's what stands out in my mind, and I know time and attention is what matters most to my own kids.

Today's Fast-Paced Lifestyles

Today life seems to run at a pace unheard of thirty years ago. I'm not sure when it happened, but everyone switched into high gear. Now most families seem to be spinning their wheels trying to keep up with everyone else, and no one is interested in slowing down.

Mike and I both love sports and are firm believers in keeping kids active. It's good for children to be involved and active, not just sitting on the couch all evening. But there's a fine line between encouraging kids to be active and running kids ragged. Many families today cross that line without even realizing it. It's a line we continuously struggle with—trying to find the perfect balance of athletic involvement for our kids and enough family and free time at home. We constantly reevaluate the activities our kids are involved in and try to keep family time a priority.

Eating on the Go

Because of the hectic schedules families keep, dinners are evolving into a fast-food frenzy, an on-the-go grab bag of food. Moms are giving up on the family dinner, and kids are paying the highest price of all.

Eating on the go

- causes overweight kids,
- can lead to eating disorders later in life,
- teaches kids family time is not important, and
- causes kids to feel disconnected from their parents.

Overweight kids. Eating on the run usually means eating fast food or takeout. Most of the food we eat this way has large amounts of sodium, sugar, and starch, increasing our calorie intake as well as our chances of being overweight. The more we eat on the go, the greater the likelihood our children will be overweight.

By sitting down to a family supper, you are seeing not only what is going into your children's mouths food wise, but you also get the opportunity to see what is coming out of their mouths conversationally. You can help them alleviate their daily stresses and add words of praise and encouragement to their lives. Kids are presented with healthy food from all the food groups, and mealtime becomes an enjoyable experience instead of a rush-around-and-stuff-something-in-your-mouth race. All in all, it may reduce the chances that your children will face eating disorders down the road and help them to maintain a healthy, balanced weight.

Eating disorders. Eating while rushing from one activity to another teaches kids an unhealthy view of food: that food is to be stuffed in our mouths as quickly as possible as we drive down the road desperately trying to get somewhere fast.

Healthy eating is eating slowly, enjoying food without emotional ties. When our children learn that mealtime can be a social, fun-filled family time, we are teaching them to have healthy eating habits that may last a lifetime and reduce their chances of developing eating disorders later in life.

Valuing family time. Eating on the go teaches our children that we don't value their time, that we don't value them. It shows kids that we would rather sprint from here to there than sit down and take the time to eat a family supper together.

Simply taking an hour each evening to sit around the dinner table together teaches our children that we value our time together, and in turn, that we value them. Increased family time leads to greater self-confidence as we fill their love tanks as well as their tummies.

Connecting kids to parents. Eating on the go reduces the number of hours we have to connect with our kids. Mealtime is social time—a time to talk about our day, share our feelings about life, and open up to one another. If we give that up, we are losing more than we realize and creating a void of silence between us and our children. On average, by the time a child graduates from high school, he or she has clocked up twenty thousand hours in front of the TV and thirteen thousand hours spent in school. Don't you want to have a bigger impact on your children than the media or their teachers? How many hours are you willing to give your children around the dinner table?

The Erosion of the Family Dinner

After years of writing and researching motherhood, best-selling author Stacy DeBroff founded www.momcentral.com, where she describes the erosion of the family dinner: "With today's hectic schedules, it can be nearly impossible to fit in family dinners into the mix of practices, lessons, and work hours that keep kids and grown-ups alike on the go."

Families aren't taking the time to eat supper together. They're running themselves and their kids ragged as they try to do it all, losing what matters most—family time.

DeBroff also discusses research conducted by the University of Minnesota that found "… in the past 20 years, there has been a 33% decline in the number of families who eat dinner together regularly." That's an amazing loss of family time, faith-building time, and time to just reconnect and create a sense of family unity. It's no wonder kids today feel disconnected from their parents, and just as many parents hardly know what is going on in their kids' lives.

Even when families try to have a family supper, it's such a challenge to find the time to prepare a nutritious meal that most settle for fast food or quick-fix meals that don't provide appropriate nutrition. DeBroff states that

- "Only 50% of American families eat dinner together every night. And 34% of these family meals come from fast-food restaurants—families grab food on the fly, relying on takeout meals as the only way to have dinner as a unit."

ADD A PINCH OF SUPPER-SWAPPING ADVICE

List all your family activities, from church choir director to volunteering in the PTA.

Have each of your kids list all of his or her activities, from soccer to piano lessons.

Have everyone in your family rank his or her own list of activities from most important to least important on a scale of one to ten.

Share your rankings with each other.

As a family, discuss which activities you could give up or postpone so

- "67% of recently surveyed families with children in organized sports said that their children's activities have changed their family's dinner routine."
- "It is estimated that American families spend almost half of their food budget on meals away from home."

The Cost of the Disappearing Dinner

With only 50 percent of American families eating dinner together regularly, kids who don't eat with their families lose a potentially strong connection to their parents. Parents find it adds to the loss of open communication between generations. Since 34 percent of the families eating dinner together are eating fast food, it also opens the door for poor eating habits and future eating disorders.

you can slow down your family evenings and make time together a priority.

For the next three months, try out your new, slower-paced schedule and see how you feel.

Use your newfound family time to do things together, like eating a more leisurely supper, playing board games, going bike riding, or just spending time hanging out doing a whole lot of nothing.

Reevaluate your decisions every few months. You can always add back an activity or two if you miss them.

Above all, don't underestimate the power of spending time together at home. Value that time. Cherish it. Make it a priority.

I have nothing against McDonald's, and yes, my kids love their chicken nuggets and french fries; but I try to limit our fast-food trips as much as possible, usually going through the drive-through on vacations or special occasions when we are out and about.

Balancing kids' activities and family time is a challenge, one every family struggles with. But dinner doesn't have to be sacrificed if you have a way to simplify meal preparation. That's where supper swapping comes in.

Every spring Mike and I struggle to fit our family supper in with his baseball coaching schedule and the kids' softball games. We're always subject to last-minute changes because of poor weather, rescheduled games, and late nights. Because eating together as a family is a priority for us, we work our mealtime around our schedules. On nights when we have games, I give the kids a small, healthy snack after school, and we head to the ball field to cheer on the Bulldogs. After the games, I bathe the kids, put them in their PJs, and help them get homework done. We eat supper when Mike gets home, usually about 7:00 or 8:00 p.m. When Mike's games go late, I eat supper with the kids and tuck them into bed myself. Mike eats when he gets home. Supper swapping won't solve all your scheduling problems. But, on those busy nights, it will give you a hot, fresh meal waiting at home.

What's important is making your family supper a priority whenever and however you can fit it in. With supper swapping, it becomes simple and allows you to make room in your life for a family meal almost every night of the week. That's the biggest blessing of supper swapping.

Dear Lord, you are amazing, and your love is never ending. Sometimes it's difficult to imagine how much you love us, how much you have sacrificed for us, and how much you care about every part of our lives, including our meals with our families. Help us to savor this time with our children and to invite you into our family and to our dinner table. As we struggle with the daily demands of life, help us to find time to be in your Word, to worship and pray to you, and to spend precious time with our family. Amen.

Potluck Activity

MEMORIES MADE

Here is a great get-to-know-you activity to share with your supper-swapping girlfriends at your next meal-planning gathering.

Take a pencil and two pieces of paper each. Don't put your name on the papers. On one sheet write down your most precious childhood memory, whether it's a treasured Christmas morning or a family vacation at Disney World. Be specific and give details. On the other sheet of paper, write down a "made up" childhood memory—something that never actually happened to you, but something someone might believe happened to you. Be as creative, humorous, and specific as you can. Pile all the papers in the center of the table. One by one, draw a paper, read it out loud, and have everyone try to guess whose memory it is and whether it's true or fictitious. Try not to fall on the floor laughing, and enjoy the stories.

Three

THE SUPPERTIME SURPRISE

The Importance of the Family Meal

Meeting Your Kids' Needs

It seems like every day my kids say or do something that catches me off guard, like a tap on the shoulder reminding me that they see our love in the details of life.

Recently, I was scheduled to speak at a mother-and-son banquet at a local church. I was planning on bringing my son Colin with me. I told him all about it—how we would get dressed

> *They worshiped together at the Temple each day, met in homes for the Lord's Supper, and shared their meals with great joy and generosity.*
> ACTS 2:46 (NLT)

up in our Sunday best and go to this wonderful, special dinner, just the two of us. His bright blue eyes grew wide with anticipation, and his smile was ear to ear.

When the day arrived, my older daughter took a tumble at school and bumped her head. We had to take her to the ER for X-rays, and, subsequently, I had to cancel attending the mother-son banquet at the last minute.

Though Colin was disappointed, he handled it well. He decided that he and I would have our own mother-and-son dinner at his favorite restaurant and then go to a movie. Every morning he asked me in his adorable six-year-old way, "Mommy, how many days until we have our date?"

Spending time with our children, especially eating together, is crucial. It means more to them than they might let on, and it shows them that they are a priority to us.

Reasons to Reclaim Your Family Supper

Having a regular family supper
- teaches your children they are a priority in your life;
- opens the door for communication between parents and children;
- helps encourage healthy eating habits and prevents eating disorders and obesity;
- helps prevent poor choices later in life, especially teenage smoking, drinking, and trying drugs; and
- gives you an opportunity to pass on your faith to your children.

I can sometimes get so caught up in my own agenda that I forget what is most important: my family. They rarely make it to my mental to-do list, rarely get prioritized in the way they deserve. I don't mentally schedule time to snuggle on the couch with my four-year-old, Riley, yet spending one-on-one time with her is so important.

I'm learning to put aside my own agenda and be what my family needs me to be. That may mean that the laundry pile grows as tall as a tree or that the dishes stay in the sink until evening or that I write my weekly newspaper column at midnight. It can be exhausting, but the payoff is worth more than a pot of gold!

Kids need to know they come first and are at the top of your to-do list. It's not always easy, but having a regular family supper is a great place to start. Family suppers can impact your kids for the rest of their lives, and supper swapping makes it simple.

Opening the Lines of Communication

When was the last time you had a heart-to-heart talk with your kids? With our busy schedules and grown-up agendas, we can sometimes spend more time talking *at* our kids than *with* our kids. Eating supper together is the perfect opportunity to give them our undivided attention, to connect with them verbally and emotionally, to speak with them heart to heart.

Our kids see how we love them in what we do more than in what we say. We can try to show it through hugs and kisses and words of affection. But more than anything, kids want your time—and it's quantity time that opens the door for quality time. There is no such thing as planned quality time. It can't be marked in ink on the calendar or scheduled during a car ride to soccer practice. The only thing that opens the door of communication with your children is being there. When you spend time with your kids, giving them your undivided attention, they will feel connected to you emotionally. And only then will they share their hearts with you.

Encouraging Healthy Eating Habits

Kids learn about food from their parents. It begins in the womb, with the only nourishment for the baby coming directly from mom, through the umbilical cord, tying them together, literally.

As infants, babies either get nourishment at their mother's breast or from a bottle, usually given by mom or dad. As you hold them close, they look up into your eyes and soak up your love as the warm milk nourishes their body. It's a wonderful beginning.

They move on to cereal, baby food, and mashed bananas. Then come Cheerios, finger foods, and anything that can be cut up small enough. As long as we're feeding them, we're right there with them when they eat. It is built-in time for love, along with nourishment.

But somewhere along the way, we forget about the love part, and eating becomes just a means to an end. We stand at the counter and chow down cold pizza. We drive through McDonald's and eat as we travel at fifty miles per hour. We let go of the connection food has to bonding and forget about the ties that bind us as we nourish our bodies.

Kids pick up on these poor eating habits, and many of these traits can root in their souls and begin a lifetime struggle with eating disorders or obesity.

There is no perfect formula that, if applied, ensures that your children will be Christian men and women, strong in their character and faith. But prioritizing your family supper will definitely give you an edge in this world filled with temptation, chaos, strife, and the numerous moral challenges your kids will face.

The National Center on Addiction and Substance Abuse at Columbia University (CASA) conducts annual surveys on teenagers and their parents to discover what makes kids say no to alcohol and drugs. In September 2005, their research once again proved how vital the family dinner is to our children's success later in life.

Ten Benefits of Frequent Family Dinners (CASA)

The more often children and teens eat dinner with their families, the less likely they are to smoke, drink, and use drugs. Children and teens who have frequent family dinners

- are at half the risk for substance abuse compared to teens who dine with their families infrequently,
- are less likely to have friends or classmates who use illicit drugs or abuse prescription drugs,
- have lower levels of tension and stress at home,
- are more likely to say their parents are proud of them,
- are more likely to say they can confide in their parents,
- are more likely to get better grades in school,
- are more likely to be emotionally content and have positive peer relationships,
- have healthier eating habits,

- are at lower risk for thoughts of suicide, and
- are less likely to try marijuana or have friends who use marijuana.

Percentage of Teens Who Smoke, Drink, Use Marijuana (by frequency of family dinners) (CASA)

	5 to 7 dinners per week	**0 to 2 dinners per week**
Cigarettes	14%	34%
Alcohol	30%	52%
Marijuana	12%	35%

Passing On Your Faith

Suppertime is faith-building time—the perfect opportunity to live out your faith not only in your words but also in your actions. As you come together around the dinner table and join hands in prayer, there are little eyes watching everything you do. They're peeking out from the corner of one eye and studying how you pray. They're learning about your faith and, hopefully, seeing God's love reflected in you.

We have taught our kids a simple, mealtime prayer they recite as we sit around the dinner table, hand in hand. It goes like this:

> God is great. God is good. And we thank him for our food.
> Through his love we all are fed; give us, Lord, our daily bread.
> Amen.

The words are simple, and the meaning is sound. I've discovered that the words aren't as important as taking the time to pray together, even with toddlers and preschoolers. What's important is that we are making a priority of thanking our creator for what he has given us.

Now that our kids are getting older, we've added a circle prayer tagged on the end. Mike begins by praying for whatever is on his heart. Then he squeezes Hannah's hand. She prays, then squeezes Colin's hand, and we go around our dinner table in a circle of faith and love.

We started this circle prayer for our older children, but we've been amazed at how the younger ones have picked it up. When the circle prayer gets to six-year-old Colin, he bows his head and recites the Lord's Prayer, word for word, except that he says, "*forget* our trespasses as we *forget* those who trespass against us" instead of "forgive." When he's done, he looks to me for a smile and a wink, which I gladly give.

I never sat and taught him the Lord's Prayer. He heard us praying it at church, and it soaked into his little spongelike heart, coming back and reflecting God's grace and love for all of us at our simple family suppers.

When the circle prayer gets to toddler Riley, she mumbles and jumbles some words together. Though we're never sure what she's saying, God knows. And when she's done, she always says, "Amen."

You can impart your faith to your children in many ways, from daily or weekly family devotions after supper to Sunday church services and Wednesday-evening Bible studies. We try to include family devotions in our routine once a week, but some weeks we don't always squeeze it in. We take our kids to church Sunday mornings, and they attend Sunday school and Vacation Bible

School. But spending time around our family dinner table discussing our faith, praying, and reading family devotions has solidified our children's faith and made it a part of our everyday lives.

When Mike and I talked about how our kids began picking up on our faith at the dinner table, he said, "Faith-building begins with us and the decisions we're making to be an active part of their lives and proactive in their faith."

Building a Winning Home Team

In his book *The Home Team: Spiritual Practices for a Winning Family*, author and father Nate Adams describes the importance of the family team and discusses twelve practices (or habits) that make a winning family. One of the most important is the act of eating together. Adams writes,

> Today millions of Christian parents are actively engaged in the life lab of raising children and seeking to provide a Christian home life. Each family is a home team and has a home court advantage that comes from God's presence and power. The reality is that most of us parents know far more than we are doing. We need help moving from the desires of our hearts and the knowledge of our heads to the disciplines of our homes.... The habit of eating together and (just as important) talking together has become one of the main practices that helps keep our home team together.

Most parents would agree that eating dinner together is an

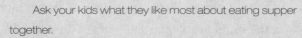

ADD A PINCH OF SUPPER-SWAPPING ADVICE

Ask your kids what they like most about eating supper together.

Talk as a family about how you can make a regular family supper a reality and how supper swapping might help you do that.

Say a simple family prayer together before each meal.

Go around the table at supper and have each person tell one good thing that happened to him or her that day.

important aspect of family life. But we don't know how to make it happen. We all want winning teams, but how do we win at the game of life? We're stuck in the vicious cycle of all the "I can'ts." But with supper swapping, families can easily move to the "I cans" and do what they already know needs to be done to have a winning family team.

That's the goal—a winning family team, winning at the game of life. That's what we're striving for. It's what we want for our kids. My hope and prayer is that my kids remember all the time we spent together sitting around our old oak dinner table talking about cardboard armadillos made from milk cartons, Valentine's Day parties, and paper Abe Lincoln hats. I hope they remember my homemade chicken pot pie, my Cheeseburger Soup, and my chocolate chip brownies. But I think I'll settle for memories of our family evenings and the time we shared together, no matter what we were eating.

 # Potluck Activity

DEFINING **M**OMENTS

Here is a great get-to-know-you activity to share with your supper-swapping girlfriends at your next meal-planning gathering.

Sit together at the kitchen table and share some of your most precious mommy memories, something one of your children said or did that you cherish, or something that still makes you laugh. Discuss why you think those memories have become defining moments in your life as a mom.

Dear Lord, thank you for the joy of family, for our loved ones and children. In their faces we see the reflection of your love. Help us to cherish and prioritize our family time, especially our family meals. As we gather together daily, be present in our hearts and at our dinner table. Amen.

Part Two

YOU NEED MORE CHEFS IN YOUR KITCHEN

Four

THE GREAT ADVENTURE

How Supper Swapping Works

The Balancing Act of Motherhood

Motherhood can sometimes feel like a circus act. As a mom, I juggle it all, usually while balancing on the tightrope of time blindfolded by the busyness of life's daily demands. I usually have five or six balls in the air at once, trying desperately not to drop one. But inevitably, life with kids makes me trip or fall, and drop all of them.

A few years back, I packed Colin, then three years old, and headed for my friend Teri's house for a morning of coffee sipping and girl talk. Teri's

> *Two are better than one, because they have a good return for their work: If one falls down, his friend can help him up.*
>
> ECCLESIASTES 4:9–10

little girl, Jae, was the same age as Colin, and so they had a regular play date as Teri and I got some girl time.

We set them up in the recreation room with toys, a kitchen play set, and enough building blocks to build a replica of the Golden Gate Bridge. Then we walked down the hall to the kitchen to catch our breath.

We could hear them chattering away as we enjoyed our mom time. Then, suddenly, we both noticed that is was awfully quiet, too quiet, in fact. Any mom will tell you, silence is a dangerous thing when there are toddlers around.

Teri and I headed back down the hall to check on them and discovered that they had decided to explore the house a bit. They had disappeared into thin air. We called their names, no response. So we began peeking in corners and bedrooms, and eventually found them in Teri's master bathroom covered from head to toe in bright red lipstick.

It was quite a sight to behold. They had painted each other's faces, arms, legs, and even clothing in red stripes. In all of about ten minutes, they had even managed to paint the carpet, a chair, and the bathroom walls and floors as well. Teri looked at me and caught my eye. We weren't sure if we should laugh or cry. I think we did both.

Then, Teri did what any good mom would do. She grabbed the camera so we could capture this Kodak moment for posterity. Once we had our snapshots, we began to scrub up the mess, which took most of the morning. We had to trade our me-time into an all-morning lipstick-scrubbing fest. But when you have kids, you do what you need to do.

Life with kids is full of insane moments, times when you can't believe the mess you're in. It's a constant stress to balance the mommy must-dos with mommy can-dos and distinguish between the two.

That's why I joined a supper-swapping group to begin with—
to help me balance it all with the help of my friends and to
simplify my supper needs so I could have more time to do what I
want to do.

How Supper Swapping Works

In a supper-swapping group, friends or neighbors prepare supper
for each other on a rotating basis, but you don't eat together. One
day a week you prepare enough dinners for everyone in your
group (one meal times four or five). You keep one of those meals
for your own family and deliver the rest to the other families in
your group. The other days of the week, supper is delivered to
your door by the other supper swappers.

Supper swapping is sometimes called co-op cooking. But supper swapping is a better term since you don't cook together—you
just swap the meals you have prepared individually.

Friends Helping Friends

Supper-swapping groups can take many forms—from friends
and neighbors to coworkers or extended family members. Any
group of people has the potential to be a successful supper-
swapping group. Your group may even change and adapt with
different members over the years.

I already shared close friendships with some women before we
began supper swapping. Other women were acquaintances who
shared the same desire to simplify their dinnertime, and through
supper swapping, we became close friends.

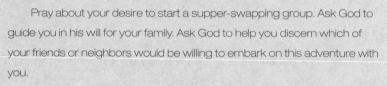

Here's how a typical week of supper swapping looks:

- Monday, Nann delivers pork chops and mashed potatoes at 5:30 p.m.
- Tuesday, Teri delivers Pasta Ham Bake and tossed salad at noon. That evening after supper, I prepare four meals of Crispy Baked Chicken and Wild Rice and put them in the refrigerator overnight.
- Wednesday, Kelly comes by at 1:00 p.m. and drops off the Cheeseburger Soup and breadsticks she has prepared for supper; at the same time she picks up the three extra Crispy Baked Chicken and Wild Rice meals I've prepared. She delivers both her soup and my chicken to Nann and Teri, keeping one chicken meal for herself. (The next week, I will

Willingness—Are you, your husband, and your kids willing to try supper swapping? What trial period will work for you?

Advantages—What immediate rewards would you see by having a regular family dinner together? What lifelong advantages would you be giving your children by eating dinner as a family every night of the week? Is that important to you? How could you use this time to strengthen your family's faith?

Possibilities—How would your life change by reducing your meal preparation by 80 percent? How would your life be impacted by adding deeper friendships with your girlfriends? How could you use supper swapping to witness to others in your community?

Supper swapping isn't a good fit for every family. Don't get discouraged if your friends are reluctant to try it. It took Teri more than a year of watching me swap meals with other friends successfully before she felt comfortable trying it out for herself.

deliver Kelly's meals and my own on Wednesday. That way we each deliver meals only two times per month.)

- Thursday, I pull out the Crispy Baked Chicken and Wild Rice, put it in the oven, and eat a wonderful supper with my family.
- Friday, we usually eat leftovers from the week's supper-swapping meals, or I make something simple like pancakes.

It's an incredible reduction in my workload, my mommy must-dos. Before swapping suppers, I was preparing five meals a week. Now, I make just one. That's an 80 percent reduction in the number of weeknight dinners I have to cook—208 fewer dinners per year to worry about!

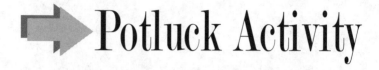

Potluck Activity

On a Roll

Here is a great get-to-know-you activity to share with your supper-swapping girlfriends at your next meal-planning gathering.

Life is full of adventures and risks—and usually Murphy's Law rules. When you try to butter the toast and scramble the eggs at the same time, the toast inevitably falls off the plate, onto the floor. Butter-side down, of course. That's just life.

Flexible Cooking

Supper swapping is as flexible as you want it to be, and it can be tailored to meet the needs of the families involved. It works well no matter what your lifestyle or daily schedule because you personalize it to meet your individual needs.

You Don't Need to Be Emeril

Over the years, I've discovered cooking really isn't that difficult, and recipes don't have to be intimidating. I don't look for

Since everyone has occasionally had silly things happen to her, start sharing. Find two dice and have each person take a turn rolling them. If the numbers rolled add up to an even number (i.e., 1+3=4), she gets to skip a turn and pass the dice on to the next player. If the numbers rolled add up to an odd number, then she must share an embarrassing story about herself with the group. Maybe she locked herself out of the house one day or forgot her mother-in-law's birthday.

Take turns going around the circle until you have no more stories to share or until you can't see straight because you're laughing so hard. Try not to snort when you laugh. Now that's embarrassing!

complex recipes to follow—I'm not Emeril—and I just don't love cooking that much. But I've found recipes that work well for my family and are easy to make. And I've found that some boxed mixes taste as good as from-scratch recipes and can save me time in the kitchen.

I've learned to balance the from-scratch recipes with the boxed mixes, the frozen bagged-up-and-boxed-up delicacies with the fresh produce. In the end, as long as the meal is prepared from the heart and shared with love, it's delicious in more ways than one.

Cooking can be as simple or as hard as you want it to be. Design your supper-swapping meals to fit your cooking style—

from gourmet chef to stressed-out mom making instant chocolate chip cookies from premade refrigerator dough. It's all up to you!

Lean on Me

When I became a mom more than a decade ago, I had no idea what my life would be like today. I wouldn't trade a minute of it; however, motherhood is exhausting at times. When I try to do it all on my own, I can run myself ragged. I need to rely on help from friends to reclaim my job as a mom whose primary responsibility is to create a nurturing home and family culture.

I may still feel overwhelmed at times by the busyness of life's daily demands, but now I have three friends helping me feed my family. On days when I lose my balance or fall flat on my face, they are there with a meal in hand, lifting me up and helping me begin again.

Dear Lord, thank you for surrounding us with your love and forgiving our self-reliances. We know that we tend to go it alone. We don't turn to you for help. We don't ask others for help. We stubbornly charge ahead amid the exhaustion and frustration, the chaos and commitment of daily life. We ask your forgiveness. Help us to turn to you and realize that we are not alone. Help us to lean on loved ones around us. As we try to simplify the small stuff and give supper swapping a try, help us to focus on the big stuff, like the love of our family and our faith in you. Amen.

Five

FROM FRAZZLED TO DAZZLED

My Supper-Swapping Story

In the Beginning

When I began swapping suppers five years ago, I had no idea where the path would lead me. Since my own supper-swapping story involves some of my dearest friends, whom I cherish, and my own precious family, I want to introduce them all to you.

> *The LORD your God will bless you in all your harvest and in all the work of your hands, and your joy will be complete.*
> DEUTERONOMY 16:15

Though I think they are some of the best people in the world, in reality they are just normal people facing challenges just like you and me. It's funny, but sometimes the most ordinary people can impact your life in the most extraordinary ways.

The Berg Clan

Mike grew up on a beef cattle farm in the same small town where we live today. He played college football (defensive tackle to be exact) at Baldwin-Wallace College and got his degree in accounting and education. Mike teaches junior high and high school math and loves being around kids of all ages. He coached football for fifteen years and has been coaching baseball for eleven.

I grew up in Olmsted Falls, a suburb of Cleveland, and am still kind of a city girl at heart. Mike and I met at B-W, where I received my degree in marketing, and were married in 1992. We live in a century-old farmhouse with hills and trees all around, and cattle right outside our kitchen window.

We have four children, three girls and a boy, ages eleven to four. Hannah is my winter child, warming our lives with her love like a blazing fire on a cold winter's night. She enjoys playing the piano, softball, and basketball. Sydney is my spring child, blossoming joy into our lives with her smile and cheerful spirit. She loves playing the piano, basketball, and finding frogs in the yard so she can set them free in the field. Colin is my summer child, filling our family with blasts and booms of fun like fireworks on a hot summer's night. He loves anything related to Star Wars or baseball. And Riley, my autumn child, keeps us hopping as she blows freely like a leaf on the wind, making her own path in this life.

Over the last decade, I have changed more than sixteen thousand diapers, wiped up countless spills of milk (and unmentionables not worth mentioning), and lost more sleep than I can recall. I wouldn't trade a moment of my mothering adventures for anything—except maybe a mocha latte on a bad day.

Annie Weaver

Annie and her husband, Steve, live a wonderful life as a farming family. They have four children, three girls and a boy, all under age ten. Annie is the kind of friend who makes you feel better about yourself. She has a true spirit of joy, is always bubbly and energetic, and makes life as a mom look simple. She is a glass-is-half-full person if I've ever known one, and she teaches me how to find the joy in the everyday. Annie is the one who introduced me to supper swapping and started the trend that led to this book.

Carla Bidlack

Carla and her husband, Broc, are busy raising four great kids. Broc is a junior high principal, and Carla is a stay-at-home mom who loves to scrapbook, make homemade cards and homemade jewelry, and do anything crafty. (Quite intimidating for someone like me with no crafting abilities whatsoever.) Before I swapped suppers with her, I didn't know Carla very well. She was one of those friends I adored from afar, someone I always wished I knew better but never found the time to get to know. Through supper swapping, Carla and I were blessed to become closer, and to this day I consider her to be one of my best friends.

Audrey Doty

Audrey and I became friends when our husbands began coaching football and baseball together over a decade ago at Dalton High School. We share the blessings and burdens of being a coach's wife and are able to support and encourage each other through each and every season. Her husband, Mike, teaches high school history and works in the summers as a contractor. Audrey is a stay-at-home mom busy raising their three adorable girls. She volunteers part-time at her church, loves scrapbooking, and teaches me how to be a person of strength and courage. I truly cherish her friendship.

Amy Frantz

Amy is one of the sweetest gals you could ever meet, soft spoken and tenderhearted. She and her husband, Matt, have four kids, including twin eight-year-old girls. Matt is a contractor, building and designing homes, and Amy is a former elementary school teacher who is now a stay-at-home mom. Amy is more than just a friend; she is family—our husbands are first cousins. Whenever we get together, we joke that the guys do more of the gabbing than we do, reminiscing about the years they played college football together or telling tales of the buck that got away last hunting season. Amy has taught me about finding the joy in motherhood, and I admire her tremendously.

Teri and her husband, Jerry, live on Teri's family's dairy farm across the road from our farm. They have three kids, one boy in high school and two younger girls. Teri and I lived as neighbors long before we became best friends. When we finally took the time to get to know each other, we discovered that we were a lot alike. (Though I love reminding her that she is older than me.) Teri is one of the most giving people I know, has a heart full of compassion, and is always doing something for someone in need. She is a stay-at-home mom who works part-time at her church and is probably one of the best cooks I know.

Nann and her husband, Mark, live with their eight-year-old son and Nann's parents. They are originally from the city of Canton and moved out to "the country" only a few years ago. Nann and Mark both work full-time managing adult-care homes for the mentally and physically handicapped. Their home is the neighborhood hang out, and they love being around kids of all ages. Nann and I met when our kids were in 4-H together, and soon after that they, along with Nann's parents, joined the church Mike and I attend. Now we share our faith as well as our meals, and we have become close friends in the process. I am blessed by her joyful, giving spirit.

Kelly and her husband, Dave, live in a beautiful wood-and-brick home that Dave built. They have three sons, all under ten years of age, and live for summer baseball season. Dave works in manufacturing, and Kelly is a stay-at-home mom who volunteers at the elementary school and is active in their church. Until we began swapping suppers together two years ago, I didn't know Kelly that well. She became friends with Nann when their boys played baseball together, and Nann invited her to join our supper-swapping group. Kelly has a kind, gentle spirit and is one of the friendliest people I know. I am so grateful that we have been able to become friends through supper swapping.

Supper-Swapping Dateline

Now that you know all about us, I want to tell you my supper-swapping tale. Sometimes, the best way to share your life is to tell your story. Once upon a time ...

Autumn 2002

My friend Annie Weaver lit the pilot light for me to start swapping suppers back in 2002. She formed a supper-swapping group after seeing a story on co-op cooking in *Better Homes and Gardens*. She shared her excitement about the simplicity and success of her group with Carla, who decided to start her own.

Carla invited Amy, Audrey, and me to form a supper-swapping group with her in the fall of 2002. Though I had never heard of supper swapping, it sounded interesting, so I decided to give it a try.

We met at a local restaurant, and—over glasses of iced tea, recipe cards in hand—we planned our first three months of meals. We learned a lot from Annie's experiences and took much of her advice and input as we formed our own group. We decided to try swapping meals for three months, after which each of us was free to drop out if it wasn't a good fit for our family. Fumbling our way through, we began swapping meals and adjusting our schedules as we went along.

We made it through the three-month trial period and loved the benefits of supper swapping. Life was good! For a while, anyway.

About a year into supper swapping, Amy decided to drop out of our group. She wanted to cook more for her family, and though she cherished our friendships, supper swapping just wasn't working well for her family or her schedule. We were all sad, and it was hard to imagine going forward without her, but we did.

We let her go without making her feel guilty for leaving. (Though we missed her Pasta Ham Bake so much, we kept that recipe as a part of our meal calendar.) Carla, Audrey, and I continued to swap meals until spring 2004.

We discovered swapping meals with three families can work well. We simply adjusted our portion sizes to allow for more leftovers to cover at least one additional evening a week.

Spring 2004

Ever since I'd begun swapping suppers, I had been begging my best friend, Teri, to join our group. For more than a year she

watched me swap meals and build deeper friendships with Carla and Audrey, and once in a while, I even delivered an extra meal to her just to tempt her to join. (I know, unfair.)

She finally decided to give it a try in the spring of 2004 and joined our group. I think I did a cartwheel in her front yard! Not just because we'd be back to four families in our group, but because I cherished my friendship with Teri and wanted her to be a part of the group, to have the built-in framework for added time together.

Carla, Audrey, Teri, and I swapped suppers until May 2004, then took the summer months off, and started up again in the fall.

As we began to organize our group to start swapping meals again, Audrey decided to drop out. We were sorry to lose her, but we all understood and respected her decision. She felt the meal planning and organization she gleaned from supper swapping had helped prepare her to cook for her own family again every night of the week.

Once again, we were back to three families, but decided to continue, since supper swapping still added simplicity and joy to our lives.

Thanksgiving 2004

Carla called me one night before Thanksgiving to let me know she was dropping out of our group. It was, I'm sure, a difficult call for her to make, and I know it was a hard call to take. Carla was the reason I tried supper swapping in the first place, and she and I had been swapping meals for over two years.

I completely understood her reasons, but my heart was broken. The tears were running down my face, though I tried not to let her know I was crying. I didn't want her to feel bad about her decision and let her go as best as I could.

Teri and I were the only ones left. We took time off over the holidays and put supper swapping in our prayers to see where God was leading us.

On Super Bowl Sunday, I was at Nann's house watching the big game and eating way too much junk food. As our husbands talked touchdowns and tackles, we sat and talked motherhood and supper swapping.

I didn't give her a sales pitch. I had almost given up on finding

Potluck Activity

STORYBOOK ENDING

Here is a great get-to-know-you activity to share with your supper-swapping girlfriends at your next meal-planning gathering.

Gather around the kitchen table and give each person a piece of paper and a pencil. Tear your paper into three pieces and number them 1-2-3. Individually, create an ending to each of these stories by completing the following sentences:

Paper No. 1: Mandy was only twenty-five years old, and she and her husband were expecting their first baby.

more families to swap meals with. However, Nann started asking me questions about it, so I shared my story with her. When she expressed an interest in swapping meals with Teri and me, I could hardly believe my ears! Teri, Nann, and I swapped meals from January 2005 through May 2005. We were settled with three families and were in a comfortable routine.

Since I was her best friend, the one she could always count on to be honest, I knew that I needed to tell her the truth, that childbirth ...

Paper No. 2: Kids can say the silliest things, things that make you laugh out loud and stop you in your tracks with their unbridled honesty. I remember when ...

Paper No. 3: The first time I met my husband, the first thought that went through my head was ...

When everyone is done, pile all of the papers in the center of the table. One by one, draw a story out and read it to the group. Try to guess who wrote it. After the author is identified, you can share more of your story with the group and elaborate on your ending.

Teri, Nann, and I were a great team, and supper swapping was going well. We took the summer months off again and planned to start when the school year began. Over the summer, Nann talked to Kelly about our group. Kelly had kids in school with ours, but none of us knew her very well. She had been in several supper-swapping groups that had fizzled out. So when she seemed interested in trying it again, we invited her to join us. She jumped right in, and the four of us have been swapping suppers ever since.

Take a Chance

I had butterflies in my stomach when Carla invited me to form a supper-swapping group with her. I was afraid to jump into something I knew nothing about. I was afraid of failing, letting my friends down, hurting someone's feelings, cooking meals no one would enjoy, or losing friendships in the process. However, I was struggling with our family suppers, and I needed help.

Supper swapping might not be what you need. But you'll never know until you give it a try. Amy tried supper swapping for about six months and then decided it wasn't a fit for her family. Audrey swapped suppers with us for more than a year before leaving our group. And Carla left after two years. But none of them regret having tried supper swapping, and each one learned something in the process.

Supper swapping does have a life cycle, and you won't swap meals for the rest of your life. Some families will swap suppers for a few months, some a few years. Whatever the time span is for your family, I guarantee you'll gain a lot from giving it a try. Don't let fear hold you back from starting something new, something that might just bless your family in ways you can hardly imagine.

Dear Lord, thank you for blessing us with a loving family and wonderful friendships. We know our work is only meaningful when we seek your will. Help us to harvest love in our homes, joy in our work, and friendship in our supper-swapping group. Grant us your grace when we forget what life is truly about and lead us in your will. Amen.

Six

RIGHT FROM THE START

How to Start Your Own Supper-Swapping Group

Take a Chance on Something New

I don't like change. I am a creature of habit, a woman who likes the status quo. When things do change, it kind of freaks me out to say the least. But at a very young age I learned that life is too short not to leap out of your comfort zone and try something new. I learned that

> In the beginning God created the heavens and the earth. Now the earth was formless and empty, darkness was over the surface of the deep, and the Spirit of God was hovering over the waters. And God said, "Let there be light," and there was light.
>
> GENESIS 1:1–3

even if you fail, you're stronger in the end. That's how we grow, by stretching our limits and trying new things.

When I graduated from high school twenty years ago (which makes me feel very old, by the way), I decided to go out of state to college, spreading my wings farther than I ever had before. I wanted something new, something that was just mine. I started off as a freshman at Allegheny College in Pennsylvania. I went there knowing absolutely no one, hoping to make new friends and build a whole new life. I remember walking down the steep hill from my dorm to the campus quad all by myself. It was a crisp autumn day and the leaves were crunching beneath my feet. I felt a lump in my throat the size of an apple, and I fought back the tears as I wondered to myself why I had moved so far away from home. There I was, all alone, trying to fit into a world where everybody seemed to know everybody else and no one wanted to take the time to get to know me.

It was a rough first semester for me, and I realized I needed my family more than I thought. I discovered that I wasn't ready yet to be completely on my own. So I left Allegheny College and moved back home to the familiar people who loved me most.

I don't regret taking that risk and moving out of state. It was a time of growth for me, a time when I discovered who I was and what I wanted in life. When I returned home, I transferred to Baldwin-Wallace College, a stone's throw away from my child-hood home. I found my niche at B-W, along with a circle of friends I came to adore.

I also met Mike there when I was a sophomore, and his love changed the course of my entire life. Mike was the one who intro-duced me to Jesus Christ. Though my Allegheny experience was a tough lesson to learn, I don't think I would be who I am today without having traveled down that path. Sometimes we have to take a risk in life—a leap of faith into the unknown—to see where God leads us.

As nervous as I was to try supper swapping, I gave it a shot because I had learned over the years that sometimes it's those leap-of-faith moments into the unknown that propel us to even greater places. I stepped out of my comfort zone to see if I truly could simplify my family dinners and discovered that I gained even more than I had ever imagined.

How to Get Started

You'll go through three basic steps to get your supper-swapping group started. First, determine how many meals a week you'd like to swap. Second, decide who you want to invite to join your group. And finally, invite those friends to try supper swapping with you.

Determine how many meals a week you want. How many families will work best to swap meals with, keeping in mind your lifestyle and specific needs? You can begin by swapping meals two nights a week with one friend and see how it works.

Next, how many nights each week would you like to have a complete supper? Usually two to five nights work best. If you swap with fewer than five families, you could each make a larger meal and use the leftovers for additional meals.

Decide who to invite to join your group. Make a list of who you want to invite for this swapping adventure. Choose families
- that are about the same size as yours, so meal sizes and portions will be about equal.
- who have similar lifestyles and compatible food tastes.
- whose cooking you've already tasted, if possible. This prevents problems down the road and eliminates hurt feelings.

- who live fairly close by, so delivery isn't an added hassle.

Invite those friends to try supper swapping with you. Once you've decided to give supper swapping a try and have recruited two to four friends, invite them over to work out the details. Don't be discouraged if you can find only one other friend interested in supper swapping. Begin swapping two nights a week with that friend, making portions large enough to have leftovers, and you'll have four weeknights covered. Pray about adding members to your group and see where God leads.

What to Bring to Your First Meeting

- Calendars or daytimers—to decide on cooking days and delivery times.
- Recipe cards or books—to choose three months' worth of meals you'll prepare (typically twelve to fifteen recipes per individual).
- Blank meal calendars—to fill in with all the details decided upon at the meeting. (See www.supperswapmom.com for free printable calendars.)
- A positive attitude and flexible agenda—try to establish your group so you meet the needs of all of the families involved.

What to Decide at Your First Meeting

1. Decision process. How will group decisions be made?
2. Time frame. How many months of meals will you plan at a time? Usually a three-month trial period works well.
3. Swapping days. How many days do you want to swap meals?

ADD A PINCH OF SUPPER-SWAPPING ADVICE

Keep it simple. Be flexible. Do what works for you.

Everything about supper swapping can be tailored to meet the needs of the group. That's why it's so successful!

Start small, with two or three families swapping for a one- to three-month trial period.

Form your supper-swapping group with families similar to yours in size, tastes, and lifestyle.

4. Delivery days and times. Who will deliver supper on what days? Will you exchange meals daily, weekly, or monthly?

5. Meal size. How many dishes constitute a meal? (We swap a main dish and a side dish or dessert, but some groups swap more. It's all up to you.)

6. Food challenges. How will you handle food allergies or dislikes?

7. Portion sizes. What pan sizes will be used? How many portions do you need? (We use 9x13-inch baking dishes for our main dish, which gives us plenty of leftovers.)

8. Meal handoff. Does someone need to be home when you deliver your meals? (You can exchange house keys, garage-door codes, or leave a cooler with ice in it on the front porch if you can't be home.)

9. Meal evaluation. How will the group evaluate the meals? Honesty is key.

10. Pans. How will you handle rotating pans through the group? Glass baking dishes with snap on lids work best. If you all

Don't try all new recipes. Use recipes your family already enjoys and simply make them in bulk to swap.

Be flexible. Try swapping meals one way, and if it doesn't work, change your methods.

Make sure to put your supper-swapping group and your decisions in prayer. Seek God's will for your families.

If your family seems uninterested in trying to swap suppers, let them know that if they're willing to try it for a month and don't like it, you will quit the group.

purchase them, there will be no issue here. (See the pan formula on page 108.)

11. Last-minute changes. How will you handle last-minute meal changes or cancellations? Should you all agree on a backup plan like switching days or ordering pizza for your group when life gets in the way? (We usually make a quick phone call if there are any meal or delivery time changes.)

12. Calendar printing. Who will print or copy and distribute the meal calendars?

13. Swapping life cycle. How will your group adapt to change when someone leaves the group? How much notice will you request when someone wants to leave?

Part of the reason supper swapping is so popular is because it's simple and can be adapted and tailored to meet your needs. No two groups need to look the same, and how you set your group up is completely up to the members of your group. The most important thing to remember as you begin this adventure is to honor

God through your words and actions, showing others love and respect. Most of all, seek God's will for the direction of your group.

 Potluck Activity

ALPHABET SOUP

Here is a great get-to-know-you activity to share with your supper-swapping girlfriends at your next meal-planning gathering.

Tear a sheet of paper into twenty-six pieces. On each piece, write down one letter of the alphabet. Fold the papers and place them in a bowl. One at a time, have each person draw a paper from the alphabet-soup bowl.

When you draw a letter, you must then describe the person sitting to your left with a characteristic or personality trait that begins with that letter. (If I draw the letter P, I might say that Teri is patient.) Rotate turns around the circle until the alphabet soup is gone—and have fun with Q and Z!

Dear Lord, it's difficult to imagine what it was like before you brought light into the world. We can hardly grasp the image of utter darkness. You created the heavens and the earth; you created us, and right from the start, you were there. You're the beginning and the end, and yet you know us by name. You care for us. You care for our families. And though our lives are full of beginnings and endings, you are our constant, never-changing love. As we begin a new adventure in supper swapping, we ask for your guidance, your grace, and your presence. We want to walk this path with you and give you thanks and praise for leading us to this new adventure. Amen.

.Seven.

CASHING IN AT THE CHECKOUT

How Supper Swapping Saves You Money

Big Spender

I used to be a shopper. I used to love shopping for clothes, food, and especially shoes. In fact, when I was in college, I had quite a shoe collection—almost a pair in every color of the rainbow. I had shoes for every occasion, from formal affairs to fishing. I had them all, including pink high tops (which I loved).

I was living at home, attending a local university, and working part-time at this job or that. I worked as a preschool teacher, a data processor, a secretary, and a dishwasher at a local

> *Honor the LORD with your wealth, with the firstfruits of all your crops; then your barns will be filled to overflowing, and your vats will brim over with new wine.*
>
> PROVERBS 3:9–10

pizza parlor. I was a jack-of-all-trades, spender-of-all-money, collector-of-all-shoes. And as most college kids do, I spent a lot of money on eating out.

I could blame my money mismanagement on my youth. I truly didn't worry about money. I was young, naive, and immature. I was raised in a middle-class home in a small suburb with sidewalks and stop signs and families struggling to pay their bills. My mom and dad probably struggled some months, but they never told us. They just paid for it all and gave us the security of knowing that they had it covered.

I never really budgeted until I had to. Like being thrown into the deep end of the pool, money management hit me after I married. Suddenly I had to pay rent, buy groceries, and somehow find enough money left over for the gas and electric bills. Talk about trying to stay afloat!

The Growing Grocery Bill

If you're like me, now that we have kids, our grocery bill keeps on mounting. From diapers to Doritos, lunchmeat to lasagna, and everything in between, our grocery bill often seems overwhelming. We're not alone in our grocery-budgeting dilemmas. In the January 2006 issue of *Money* magazine, editor-at-large Jean Chatzky writes,

> Grocery shopping seems simple enough, but Americans are wasting more money, food, and time than ever by not planning. We spend more on food each year (an average of $5,340 these days) than on anything else besides our house and car. We research the purchases of homes and cars exhaustively

before buying because we know that the bigger the line item,
the greater the opportunity to save. Can't we spend ten minutes on a grocery list?

Before I began supper swapping, I was one of those unorga-
nized people wasting money at the grocery store. Later in the
Money magazine article, Phil Lempert of Supermarketguru.com,
which tracks the industry, stated, "When we don't plan, we buy
the wrong things, which causes us to spend more money and
time." In fact, families today are tossing out 14 percent of the food
they purchase as wasted leftovers, rotten produce, or outdated
food. (That's double what our parents threw out twenty years ago!)

If we can stop throwing away that 14 percent by buying only
what we will eventually use, based on national averages we can
presumably save about $750 a year on our grocery bill. If we then
save an additional $50 a month on purchases through supper
swapping, we save an additional $600. That's a total savings of
about $1,350 per year!

Saving at the Grocery Store

Experts agree that saving at the store requires a little more
preparation, but you'll benefit in the long run.

Buy in bulk. When you grocery shop, try to buy your ingredients in bulk. If you need four pounds of ground beef or chicken, it
might be cheaper to buy the large five-pound pack instead of four
one-pound packs. Even though you end up with an extra pound, it
will save you money in the long run, and you can use the extra
meat to make a meal to share with a neighbor or freeze it to use
on a nonswapping night.

Plan ahead. Make a list of your pantry staples—things you always have on hand for breakfasts, lunches, and snacks. Then, add your supper-swapping meal ingredients for the next few months to that list. As you shop each week, you can easily buy your staples and also check your meal-ingredient list. If anything is on sale, buy it ahead to store in your pantry or freezer. When you buy an item, put a check mark next to it on your master list so you won't overbuy and waste food.

One grocery store where I like to shop occasionally has "buy one, get one for a penny" or "buy five for $19.95" meat deals. When that occurs, I purchase ahead and freeze the meat for later use, saving up to 50 percent.

Meal Cost Example: Lasagna and Garlic Bread

Ingredients	Cost*	Amount	Per Family Meal Cost
Lasagna Noodles	$1.06/Box	1/2 box per family	$.53
Parmesan Cheese	$2.27/Can	1/2 canister per family	$1.14
Mozzarella Cheese	$6.42/Bag	1/5 bag per family	$1.28
Ricotta Cheese	$2.53/Can	1/2 can per family	$1.27
Eggs	$1.28/Dozen	4 eggs per family	$0.32
Spaghetti Sauce	$1.00/Jar	1 jar per family	$1.00
Ground Beef	$13.11/6 lbs.	2 1/2 lbs. per family	$3.28
Frozen Garlic Bread	$1.74/Loaf	1 loaf per family	$1.74

Total Cost per Family Meal for a Family of 6 $10.56

Total Weekly Supper Expenditures for a Supper-Swapping
    Group with a Total of 4 Families $42.24

*Based on Wal-Mart prices in January 2006

Budget meals. Meals will vary in cost, and there's no easy way to track equality of spending, nor should you try. You can, however, decide on a ballpark figure for your supper-swapping meals, like $30–$60 for a week's meals. Try not to make meals that are too expensive or too cheap. Agree at the outset on what you expect the meals to cost.

We each try to balance our monthly grocery bill by not swapping more than two pricier meals a month. We all prefer boneless, skinless chicken breasts, which is a more expensive meat. So if I am making Crispy Baked Chicken one week for the group, the next week I'll balance that with something fairly inexpensive, like lasagna.

Supper-Swapping Meal Costs

	Low	Midlevel	High
Weekly Spending on Supper-Swapping Meals	$20	$40	$60
Per Meal Cost* (four families/four meals)	$5	$10	$15

*Each meal includes main dish and one side dish and serves a family of six.

Depending on the meals you choose to swap, how many are in your group, and the portion sizes you determine will work best for your families, you can expect to spend anywhere from $20–$60 a week on your supper-swapping meals. That works out to an average of $.83–$2.50 per person per meal. That's a huge savings over quick-fix meals and fast food.

Type of Supper (serves family of 6)	Per Meal Cost	Per Person/ Per Meal Cost
Ordering Pizza* (serves family of 6)	$24.00	$4.00
Fast Food/Takeout** (serves family of 6)	$25.00	$4.17
Dream Dinners or Dinners by Design (serves family of 4)	$16.67	$4.17
Supper Swapping (serves family of 6)	$5.00–$15.00	$0.83–$2.50

*Based on average of two large pizzas from Pizza Hut and Papa Johns
**Based on average fast-food prices of four kids meals and two adult meals

Better Nutrition with Supper Swapping

Most pizza or takeout is very high in sodium, fat, and sugars. These and similar meals are a quick fix for hunger but have poor nutritional value. An article titled "Survey Links Fast Food, Poor Nutrition Among U.S. Children" on the U.S. Department of Agriculture Web site discusses research that found that "U.S. children who ate fast food, compared with those who did not, consumed more total calories, more calories per gram of food, more total and saturated fat, more total carbohydrates, more added sugars, and more sugar sweetened beverages, but less milk, fiber, fruit and nonstarchy vegetables."

The research also proved childhood consumption of fast food increased fivefold from the 1970s to the 1990s, at the same time childhood obesity increased. Most parents want their children to eat healthy meals, but wanting something and knowing how to accomplish it are two different things. Supper swapping gives parents exactly what they need to help their children eat healthier, by decreasing their consumption of fast food and increasing their consumption of home-cooked meals.

Other Meal-Simplification Techniques

The book *Once-a-Month Cooking* by Mary Beth Lagerborg and Mimi Wilson was the original meal-simplification book. It has been a phenomenal success in presenting a way to simplify suppers by spending one day a month cooking, then freezing all those meals for later use. You can even join with a girlfriend or two, make your monthly freezer meals in bulk and then swap them to combine the best of both methods.

For many families, cooking once a month was a blessing that did solve their dinnertime dilemma. It certainly was a hot trend, and today several retail franchises have capitalized on this method of meal simplification.

Dream Dinners and Dinner by Design, to name just two, offer a month's worth of meals that you can preorder from their Web sites. You then attend a two-hour work session at their retail kitchen store to prepare those meals. When you show up, they have all the ingredients ready, and all you do is assemble your meals in freezer containers that they provide and head home with a trunk full of food.

For your two hours of meal preparation and a cost of two hundred dollars or more, you walk away with twelve meals to freeze for the month. Though it is more expensive than supper swapping, it's a great option for moms who want the simplicity of supper swapping or once-a-month cooking without the mess and hassle of making it in their own kitchen.

Whether you choose to cook once a month for yourself, purchase your meals at a retail location, or form your own supper-swapping group, the most important thing is that you come to the table daily with your family to enjoy dinner. Discover what meal-simplification method works best for your family's style, schedule, and budget; and add the most important ingredient of all … love.

Financial Gains

Supper swapping equips you with the tools you need to serve home-cooked meals to your family at a very low cost. The per-person, per-meal cost savings can add up over time. If you order pizza or takeout three times a week, spending approximately $25 each time:

$25.00 x 3 = $75.00 per week

$75.00 x 4.5 weeks per month = $337.50 per month

$337.50 x 12 months per year = $4,050 annual spending

After one year of supper swapping, you can potentially save $4,000 if you completely cut out fast food and delivered pizza. Even if you cut it in half, that's still an annual savings of almost $2,000!

Leftover Luxury

Mike is a pretty picky eater, a meat-and-potatoes man, and so I was a little nervous when I first joined a supper-swapping group.

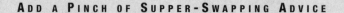

Add a Pinch of Supper-Swapping Advice

After you plan your meal calendars, write down your individual meals and the needed ingredients on a sheet of paper and tuck it in your purse or wallet. As you shop over the next few weeks, check that list and see if it is on sale. If you can stock up on ingredients when they're on sale, you'll save even more money at the checkout.

Watch newspaper sales ads, especially for more expensive meats like chicken, pork, or pot roast. When these meats go on sale, and you can use them in an upcoming recipe, stock up.

Don't try to "out do" your girlfriends with fancy, expensive meals all made from scratch to prove you're a great cook. Agree at the outset that this isn't a cooking competition.

But he was kind enough to give it a try, and as a result he has expanded his tastes and enjoys almost all of the meals.

He also has been blessed with leftovers to enjoy the next day. He actually will eat whatever we had for supper for breakfast the next morning! There are some mornings when the aroma of lasagna at 6:30 a.m. wakes me from a deep sleep, and I just about gag. But it works for him, so who am I to argue?

Mike also packs leftovers for his lunch, as do most of the men in our supper-swapping group. Since Mike is a teacher, his other option would be to purchase a school lunch. He saves time not having to put together a lunch, and he eats a more nutritious meal than cold lunchmeat or PB and J. In addition, he saves us money by not buying his lunch. And these savings add up.

Keep your recipes simple. I even use store-bought meatballs from the freezer section instead of buying ground beef, and I actually save money. The taste? Well, they taste awesome, especially in my Meatballs and Sausage recipe.

Start with fairly inexpensive meals your family enjoys. There is nothing wrong with casseroles, spaghetti, or soups.

You may want to track what you're currently spending on your suppers and use that as a cost ceiling. You definitely don't want to spend more while supper swapping than you did prior.

Try not to schedule two expensive meals back-to-back in the same month. Spread them out over time.

Replacing School Lunches

School lunches for adults at $2.10 x 5 days a week = $10.50 a week

$10.50 x 4.5 weeks a month (approx.) = $47.25 per month

$47.25 x 9 months of school = $425.25

Wow! Mike packing leftovers saves us about $425 per year in meal expenses, and that's only for inexpensive school lunches!

Even fast-food meals can cost about $5–$7 per person, and they usually aren't very healthy. If you or your husband work outside of the home and you've been eating out for lunch, trade that habit for packing leftovers from your supper-swapping meals. You can save a lot of money!

Replacing Eating Out

Meals cost approximately $7.00 per day x 5 days a week = $35.00 a week

$35.00 a week x 52 weeks a year =$1,820 a year

If you were eating out for your lunch every day and spending around $7, you could potentially save almost $2,000 a year!

The Big Picture

When you look at the financial gains from supper swapping, it's incredible! I knew we were saving money, but when I sat down and crunched the numbers, I was stunned. The first thing I did was call Kelly to share the great news with her. She loved hearing it, but wasn't surprised. She had seen similar savings firsthand.

Dear Lord, we realize we can get caught up in meeting our own needs and spending money our way, sometimes even spending our wealth frivolously. We want to honor you with our wealth, to live out our faith through our finances. Help us to live within our means, nourish our family, and budget our grocery bill so we teach our children how to honor you as we live our faith in all we do. Amen.

 # Potluck Activity

SPEND THRIFT

Here is a great get-to-know-you activity to share with your supper-swapping girlfriends at your next meal-planning gathering.

Have each person get out two sheets of paper. On one paper write down the most expensive piece of clothing you ever purchased. Describe what it looked like, where you wore it, and what it cost. On the other paper list the best clothing bargain you ever found. Describe what it was and how much it cost. Don't write your name on the papers. Fold them individually, put them in the center of the table, and randomly draw one out. Take turns reading them out loud and see if you can guess who spent how much on what.

Eight

FROM THE SIDELINES

What Dads and Kids Say about Supper Swapping

God's Family Plan

God created families to be unique: to have individuals come together and become stronger as a team than they would be alone. Everyone has a unique role to fill.

> *A wife of noble character is her husband's crown.*
> PROVERBS 12:4

Dad's Top Five Family Responsibilities
1. Love and honor his wife and children.

> Husbands, love your wives, just as Christ loved the church and gave himself up for her. (Eph. 5:25)

Dear friends, let us love one another, for love comes from God. Everyone who loves has been born of God and knows God. (1 John 4:7)

2. Lead his family by example.

The righteous man leads a blameless life; blessed are his children after him. (Prov. 20:7)

3. Build his house on the wisdom of God.

By wisdom, a house is built, and through understanding it is established; through knowledge its rooms are filled with rare and beautiful treasures. (Prov. 24:3–4)

4. Honor the Lord with his wealth and provide for his family.

Honor the LORD with your wealth, with the firstfruits of all your crops; then your barns will be filled to overflowing, and your vats will brim over with new wine. (Prov. 3:9–10)

5. Teach God's Word to his children.

Fix these words of mine in your hearts and minds; tie them as symbols on your hands and bind them on your foreheads. Teach them to your children, talking about them when you sit at home and when you walk along the road, when you lie down and when you get up. (Deut. 11:18–19)

Having time to communicate can be difficult for hardworking dads. Making the family suppertime a regular commitment opens the door for men to feel more connected to their families. Supper swapping makes that easier to accomplish this.

Love and honor his wife and children. Mike is not a chef, but he does make a mean omelet on Saturday mornings. Even though he doesn't cook a lot, one of the biggest gifts Mike gave me was encouragement to try supper swapping. It might not have been as romantic as a dozen roses, but it reflected his love for me and our children because he was willing to step out of his comfort zone and try something new.

Lead his family by example. Mike is the head of our home, the leader of our flock. He takes this role very seriously, and so do I. Our kids see what he does much more than they hear what he says, so it is vital that he leads our family by setting a good example of a Christian life.

God wants men to lead a blameless life and says that leading such a life blesses their children (Prov. 20:7). Though no husband is perfect, ensuring that dinner is an important part of family life is one way men can lead by example.

Since our family has been part of the supper-swapping group, Mike has more relaxed time with our children in the evenings after work and at the dinner table. He takes the lead and holds family devotions after supper one evening a week and spends time talking, listening, and leading our children in the direction he wants them to go in life.

Build his house on the wisdom of God. Mike knows how vital his faith is to his fathering. You can tell your kids you love the Lord, but if you don't live out your faith in little and big ways, they get a mixed message.

Our kids will ask Mike to pray at the dinner table. They will imitate his prayers and follow his lead. They seek out his attention and spill their day's events all at the dinner table.

Before we began supper swapping, getting dinner on the table was such a challenge that we didn't always take the time to eat a family supper, and Mike didn't have the special table-talk time with the kids. Supper swapping simplifies the dinner process so much that it makes it possible for dads to have that time with their kids to truly teach them God's wisdom. It is just one tool that gives dads more opportunities to live out their faith.

Honor the Lord with his wealth and provide for his family. Mike works full-time and provides financially for all of our family's needs. But I am the grocery shopper in our family. In fact, I can probably count on one hand the number of times Mike has gone shopping. But Mike's encouragement and support of my supper-swapping venture is one way he helps our family to honor the Lord with our wealth since we save money on our grocery bill and eat out much less.

Teach God's Word to your children. We have tried daily devotions with our kids, but sometimes we fall behind. Like most families, we can find it challenging to squeeze God's Word into our busy lives. But God wants us to do just that.

Supper swapping makes dinnertime easy and your evenings less stressful so you have more time to have family devotions. After supper is the perfect time to talk to your children about God. Having regular family meals also opens the door for dads to take the lead on reading family devotions at the dinner table when you have your kids' undivided attention. Add in a sweet treat for dessert, and you'll hold their attention even longer!

Supper swapping sounds strange to dads. Like being thrown into a new game, they don't quite "get" the rules. They may feel like staying in the locker room and not getting in the game of supper swapping. It's a new-enough concept for moms to ponder, but for dads it's even more challenging.

That's exactly what Broc (Carla's husband) thought when she first mentioned swapping suppers. He was concerned and not sure he wanted to try it.

"I didn't know if I wanted to eat someone else's food. It sounded strange to be trading food with other families," he says now.

Carla understood his reluctance and assured him they would try it out for a few months to see if they liked it before committing long-term.

Before too long, Broc was a supper-swapping fan. "Supper swapping was pretty cool because it improved our family dinnertime," he said. "It simplified our evenings, creating a more relaxed environment for our kids."

Top Five Reasons Dads Love Supper Swapping

On top of helping dads fulfill their spiritual role in the family, supper swapping also has some practical advantages for them.

More wonderful suppers. How many evenings do you throw your hands up in the air and just serve cold cereal or grilled cheese sandwiches to your family? There's nothing wrong with doing that on occasion. The problem is when it becomes the main fare.

There is something to be said about winning a man's heart by way of his stomach. I know my husband loves to sit down and eat a hearty meal that's fresh out of the oven. One huge benefit dads see from supper swapping is being blessed with more complete dinners, more wonderful recipes to savor.

A regular dinnertime. Supper swapping has helped our family keep to a regular routine even with our crazy fall and spring schedules, which Mike really appreciates. It allows us to stay focused on our family and connected to the kids, which helps give them an advantage in life.

Though we don't always get it right, we do our best, and we have created a fairly consistent routine our kids count on. As busy as life gets, we come together at the end of the day around the dinner table. On the occasional nights when we can't eat supper together, inevitably one of the kids will ask, "Aren't we eating supper together?" That simple question tells me how important our regular family suppertime routine is to them.

Wife's cooking improved. Is this a joke? How does cooking less improve our cooking? Amazingly, as we put more time into one weekly meal, we're able to fine-tune our cooking skills and try new recipes. Supper swapping gives us the chance to expand our cooking horizons with the support of our swapping group.

Before I started supper swapping I had a short list of recipes that I made for supper: meatloaf, ham, spaghetti, pot roast, stew, and a few soups. Other than that, I settled for mac and cheese, grilled cheese, or something from a can or the freezer. I rarely tried anything new, and our meals were often dull.

Joining a supper-swapping group encouraged me to taste and try new recipes, and it added variety to our lives. Mike has really enjoyed some of these new taste adventures. When our group gets together to plan meals, we bring our recipe cards, magazine clippings, and even cookbooks that have been gathering dust on our

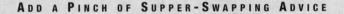

ADD A PINCH OF SUPPER-SWAPPING ADVICE

Be sure not to leave your husband out of your decision process. He may or may not be the cook in the family, but what you eat for supper impacts him as much as you. Ask his opinion. Include his input.

Once you and your husband have decided to embark on the supper-swapping adventure, discuss it with your kids. Explain what will happen and how your family dinnertime will improve.

Ask your husband what recipes he'd like to see you make for the supper-swapping group.

shelves. We try to mix in two or three old family favorites with one or two new recipes in a given week. That way, if a recipe is a flop, we still have some great meals to look forward to.

More relaxed evenings. Mike walked in the door and could immediately tell I was at my kid limit. The noise level in our home was probably close to that of a hockey game. Kids were running in and out of the kitchen, mostly fighting or tattling on each other. My head was throbbing, my eyes were rolling, and I was seriously considering a last-minute trip to Jamaica.

I was trying to get supper in the oven, help my two older girls with their homework, and keep my preschoolers out of trouble. I'm not sure how many evenings I spent like that, trying to catch my breath and not lose my mind. And I'm sure that's not what Mike wanted to come home to. But that was before I began supper swapping.

Supper swapping might not eliminate all evening chaos, but it will certainly reduce the stress level. It eliminates the

Ask your kids what their favorite family recipes are.

Invite your husband to participate when you have your meal-planning sessions. (Our husbands never seemed interested in coming to our meetings. They just like to ask for their favorite recipes to be repeated. But you can never go wrong by inviting them.)

Remember that your decision to swap suppers is a team decision. Don't make the decision alone.

hurry-up-and-get-something-in-the-oven rush that sends my head spinning. Now all I have to do is reach in the fridge and pull out that evening's main dish and side dish that had been delivered earlier in the day. I preheat the oven, put in the pans, and voila. A two-step solution to my dinnertime dilemma.

The kids usually help me set the table, and we typically add a vegetable, tossed salad, or loaf of bread to complete the meal. As simple as that, I can get supper started and then concentrate on helping my girls with their homework. I may still have a toddler to occupy, but it's a lot less chaotic when Mike walks in.

Leftovers for lunch. One thing I don't like to think about is packing lunches for Mike. Being a teacher, he used to buy school lunches, but when he discovered that they were high in fat and starches, he decided to pack. Before supper swapping, that created additional stress for me trying to come up with something to pack in his lunch. Now, it's as simple as putting leftovers together after supper.

Potluck Activity

As we clean up the kitchen and load the dishwasher, we pack Mike's lunch. He gets to enjoy delicious homemade lunches with no added cost, and my stress levels goes down. It's a win-win situation. And we end up saving money—over forty dollars a month!

The Kids' Perspective

Do kids care who made supper? As I was gathering thoughts from my family on our supper-swapping experiences, I decided to go straight to the source of all things truthful: the kids.

- One thing your family does that shows how much they love you

After you've shared your answers, say a prayer for your family members, mentioning each by name. Before you leave, each of you decides on one thing you can do for your family this week. Make it something special, like writing a love note to your husband, getting up early to make the kids pancakes for breakfast, or surprising them with a night at the movies. Share your ideas with the group, and then go to it! Surprise your family with something special, something they don't expect but will treasure in their hearts.

"Sydney," I asked my eight-year-old, "What do you like about our family being in a supper-swapping group?"

"I'm in a supper-swapping group?" she asked.

"Yep," I said, "You know how on some days mom cooks, and other days Nann, Kelly, and Teri deliver supper to us?"

"Why is that special?" she asked.

At first, I was surprised that she hadn't realized that we were a part of a supper-swapping group. But the more I thought about her reaction, the more it made sense. I started swapping suppers when Sydney had just turned five. All she knows is supper swapping. She probably thought everyone swaps meals.

Furthermore, kids don't care who prepares the meal. They only care about two things: Does the food taste good? And do we eat supper together as a family?

That's it. That's what's important to kids. Just the basics, the core of the family meal. Leave it to Sydney to help me realize what's important about supper swapping. Not the food. Not the simplicity. Not even the awesome friendships. Nope. To her, it's all about eating good food and getting to have time with Mom and Dad. Wow. It put a whole new perspective on supper swapping for me.

Dear Lord, we thank you and praise you for the gift of our husbands and children and for making us wives and moms. We know life's daily demands sometimes drag us down, and we can easily get exhausted and frustrated. We ask you to grant us forgiveness when we falter, when we lose our temper too easily and are impatient with the ones we love the most. Please help us each to be the wife and mom you intended—a "wife of noble character"— honoring you in all we say and do. As we seek to simplify our family supper through supper swapping, guide us to seek our family's input, and take their thoughts and opinions to heart. Amen.

Part Three

TROUBLESHOOTING
IN THE COMMUNITY
KITCHEN

Nine

SUPERSIZING YOUR MEALS

One Portion Size

Does Not Fit All

The Perfect Pan

Rust is never a good thing. Even the Tin Man in *The Wizard of Oz* knew that. Rust means something has been exposed to the elements or is getting old.

When my very first supper-swapping group launched, we decided not to invest a lot of money in new pans. But we also thought it would make swapping meals simpler to have pans identical in size and

> *God will meet all your needs according to his glorious riches in Christ Jesus.*
> PHILIPPIANS 4:19

style. We decided we would each contribute twenty dollars and try to get four pans each for a total of sixteen pans. As I began to shop around, it became clear that we had underbudgeted the cost. So I purchased what I thought were basic metal pans, ones that would last a year or so, though they certainly would not be family heirlooms. We decided to just cover the pans with aluminum foil for meal delivery.

Pan problem one: rust stains. The first problem we encountered was that the pans were cheaply made. They rusted in the dishwasher after the first use and didn't clean well by hand either. We were constantly trying to scrub rust stains off the pans to make them useable, which added more work than we had planned on.

Pan problem two: no lids. Because we chose to use aluminum foil instead of buying pans with lids, Murphy's Law, which states that whatever might go wrong probably will, came into play. We each had numerous spills during meal delivery, covering our car floors with sauces and toppings of all sorts. Again, this increased our workload since we now had to clean carpets.

Pan problem three: size. The 8x8-inch pans we purchased were too small for many of our meals, causing more spills and more frustration.

We had purchased those cheap metal pans because we didn't want to invest a lot up front since we weren't sure how long we would swap suppers and because we wanted to prevent pan-trading dilemmas. But we discovered that metal pans weren't the solution. So we each bought three or four 9x13-inch quality glass baking dishes with snap-on lids and used those to swap meals. Though it was a little more expensive up front, we discovered it was worth the initial investment—saving time, money, and stress down the road.

Although we mainly use the same glass baking dishes, we also use other pans and plastic containers at times, depending on the meal we're making. If we're swapping soup or stew, those whale-of-a-pail ice-cream buckets work great. You can also buy semidisposable storage containers for very little money and save your nicer plastic for other uses.

There's no easy way to make sure everyone gets her own pans returned right away, and you shouldn't try—it's too stressful. What we do is all use the same glass baking dishes and just rotate them through the group. If we do use a special container, like for a salad dressing or sauce, we label it with our name and return labeled pans when we deliver our next meal. If we have accumulated others' pans, we trade back at our meal-planning meetings. If everyone in your group is respectful and relaxed about pan trading, it won't be an issue.

Preventing Pan-demonium

1. Don't expect to get your pans or containers returned to you.
2. Only swap meals in pans or containers you're willing to share.
3. Label your pans or containers with a permanent marker if you want them returned eventually.
4. Swap pans and containers back at your quarterly meal-planning meetings.
5. Overall, remain relaxed and respectful about pans and containers.

How Many Quality Pans Do You Need?

Supper swapping means swapping pans. And since you want to avoid delivery mishaps and spills, it is wise to begin with sturdy,

9x13-inch glass baking dishes with the snap-on lids. But quality does not come cheap. So how much should you invest in your pans? Well, here is a simple formula you can use:

	Five Family Group	Four Family Group	Three Family Group
Mom #1 (Monday)	4	3	2
Mom #2 (Tuesday)	3	2	1
Mom #3 (Wednesday)	2	1	0
Mom #4 (Thursday)	1	0	
Mom #5 (Friday)	0		
Total New Pans Needed	10	6	3
Estimated Pan Cost	$120.00	$72.00	$36.00
Per Mom Pan Cost	$24.00	$18.00	$12.00

For example, if you have four families in your supper-swapping group, Mom #1 (Monday's meal) will need three new pans. She will make four meals total, but can make the meal she is keeping in one of her own pans, and deliver the other three to the group in new glass pans with lids.

Mom #2 (Tuesday's meal) will receive a new pan from Mom #1 on Monday, so she will need only two new pans for delivery (using her own pans for her own meal again). Mom #3 (Wednesday's meal) will have already received two new pans from Monday and Tuesday's meals, so she will need only one new pan (using her own pans for her own meal again).

Mom #4 (Thursday's meal) will have received three new pans from the meals that were already delivered to her Monday through Wednesday, so she will not need any new pans (using her own pans for her own meal again).

If there are four families in your group, you therefore will need a total of only six new glass baking pans and can divide the total cost between all the cooks. The glass baking pans with lids typically cost around twelve dollars, so your total group cost would be the pan cost divided by the number of cooks in the group. And for all those great sides or desserts, we use semidisposable containers or smaller glass pans. And for soups and stews, we use ice-cream tubs. All in all, you can get started with very little up-front investment and financial strain.

Healthy Food and Practical Portions

We just had a new Wendy's restaurant open up in our small town. It's exciting for someone like me who loves stuffed baked potatoes, not to mention frosty desserts. On its opening day, I couldn't resist—I just had to drive through and get some lunch. All I wanted was a small burger, no fries, no drink. But of course, I was asked, "Do you want a Biggie Size fries with that?" (McDonald's must own the copyright to the term *Supersize*.) I replied, "No, thank you," and chuckled to myself. When did a normal-size order become too small for us? When did fries become a must with every sandwich? We seem to be supersizing everything, including our waistlines!

The United States Department of Agriculture (USDA) researches American eating habits and makes recommendations on foods and portion sizes. According to its Web site (www.nal.usda.gov), "Increased intakes of fruits, vegetables, whole grains, and fat-free or low-fat milk and milk products are likely to have important health benefits for most Americans.... Although associations have been identified between specific food groups (e.g., fruits and vegetables) and reduced risk for chronic diseases, the effects are interrelated and the health benefits should be considered in the context of an overall healthy diet that does not exceed calorie needs." Another USDA Web site (www.health.gov) provides key nutritional recommendations.

USDA Key Nutrition Recommendations for Adults

- Consume approximately 2 cups of fruit and 2 1/2 cups of vegetables per day.
- Choose a variety of fruits and vegetables each day: dark green, orange, legumes, starchy vegetables, and other vegetables.
- Consume 3-ounce equivalents or more of whole-grain products per day.
- Consume 3 cups per day of fat-free or low-fat milk or equivalent milk products.

USDA Key Nutrition Recommendations for Kids

- Consume whole-grain products often; at least half the grains should be whole grains.
- Children two to eight years old should consume 2 cups per day of fat-free or low-fat milk or equivalent milk products.
- Children nine years of age and older should consume 3 cups per day of fat-free or low-fat milk or equivalent milk products.

In our supper-swapping group, we use some lower-fat ingredients, like low-fat sour cream or cheese, and we try to include fruits and vegetables as side dishes. But as far as portions go, we enjoy swapping larger-size meals since we can eat leftovers for lunch the next day or make an additional meal out of leftovers on Friday night.

As a group, you need to decide what size portions you will

swap. As a family, you can then decide how much to eat. These are separate issues. You don't have to supersize your waistline by supersizing your meals. It's all up to you! Eating smaller amounts of the food you already eat can lower your total calorie intake and help you lose weight.

Healthy Eating and the Pyramid

Whenever I take one of my children to the pediatrician for an annual checkup, the nurse always runs through a laundry list of questions, including their eating habits. The scenario always goes something like this:

> **Nurse:** Is Riley eating plenty of fruits and vegetables on a daily basis?
>
> **Me:** What do you mean by vegetables?
>
> **Nurse:** Broccoli, carrots, green beans ...
>
> **Me (laughing out loud):** Do french fries count?
>
> **Nurse:** Nope.
>
> **Me (feeling embarrassed):** Well, I try to get her to eat vegetables, though I'm not sure many actually make it into her digestive system.
>
> **Nurse:** Would you say Riley eats a well-rounded diet?
>
> **Me (accepting defeat, humbly, head hanging low):** Yes, for a three-year-old it is well rounded.

As moms, all we can do is our best, whatever that is at the moment. We can't force-feed our children. But what we can do is offer healthy food and limit unhealthy choices. If we don't have cookies in the pantry, the kids can't eat them. I'm not saying you should give up everything that tastes good and never let your kids eat cookies, but it's all about balance.

When Mike and I were first married, we drank a lot of pop. Then one day we realized how unhealthy it was and decided to make a change. So we gave it up. Now we drink water, milk, or orange juice. We don't keep fruit punch or sweetened iced tea in the house. When we eat out, we order water for us and the kids. In fact, we've discovered the more water we drink, the more water we crave. The kids have adapted to drinking water with every meal except supper, when they drink milk. Don't underestimate kids' ability to adapt to new eating habits. They will.

Though we're healthy, Mike and I aren't in perfect shape. I have some weight to lose and am trying to do that by eating smaller portions and exercising. Mike works out with his baseball team and jogs a few times a week in the warmer months. It's a lifelong struggle for us, one many parents face. I'll never be a size four. But I can definitely be a healthier me. Healthy living is about balance, and you can begin by balancing your suppers with more fruits and vegetables and fewer calories.

You can go to www.mypyramid.gov; enter your age, gender, and activity level; and create your own personal food pyramid free. This food pyramid will give you basic guidelines to eating healthier in a format that fits your lifestyle.

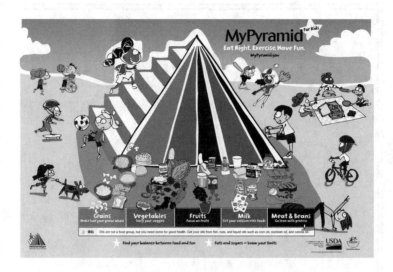

Practical Portions for Better Health

- Determine pan size for meals. Typically 8x8- or 9x13-inch works best for a main dish depending on family size.
- Determine how you can incorporate fresh fruit and vegetables in your meals as sides and desserts.
- Every quarter, reevaluate meal-portion sizes and adapt them as needed.
- If you end up throwing away leftovers after they're too old to eat, you need to reduce your meal-portion sizes.

Scrumptious Sides

Fruits and vegetables are vital to a healthy diet, and, according to the American Cancer Society Web site, eating more fruits and vegetables may even help prevent cancer. It's easier than you might think to get your daily servings in. Serving sizes are small, and you can keep it as simple as you like.

One Serving of Fresh Fruit or Vegetables

- medium apple or orange: the size of a tennis ball
- 1 cup chopped raw vegetables or fruit: baseball size
- 1/4 cup dried fruit (raisins, apricots, mango): a small handful
- lunch-box-size (single-serving size) container of unsweetened applesauce
- cup of lettuce: four leaves

- chicken stir-fry with 1 cup of mixed broccoli, carrots, and mushrooms (equals 2 vegetable servings)
- 1/2 cup cooked or canned legumes (beans and peas)
- 5 to 6 baby carrots

You can add depth to your meals by adding fresh fruit for dessert or fresh broccoli as a side dish. You can also keep these foods on hand yourself to add to meals that do not include them. If your swapping group is delivering lasagna and bread, you can easily add a fresh vegetable for a side or cut up an apple for dessert. It's not important how you include fruits and vegetables, just that you do include them.

Potluck Activity

A DESERTED ISLAND

Here is a great get-to-know-you activity to share with your supper-swapping girlfriends at your next meal-planning gathering.

Have each person take a sheet of paper and write answers to the following questions:

1. If you were stranded alone on a deserted island and could have only three things with you, what would they be?

2. While on that island, you must eat the same food every day. What food would you choose?

3. Would you try to get off of the island by building a raft and heading out to sea or would you adapt by making a new home for yourself there?

Dear Lord, thank you for blessing us with plenty of food to eat, a home to live in, and sometimes even sweet treats for dessert. Everything we have comes from you, and we praise you for blessing us beyond our wildest dreams. Help us to use wisely what you have given us. As you meet our needs, nourishing our families, remind us to share our blessings with those around us, our neighbors and friends, and even perfect strangers you put before us each day. Amen.

• Ten •

THE LIGHTER SIDE

Surviving Supper-Swapping Mishaps with Your Sanity Intact

Learning to Laugh at Life's Mishaps

I think God allows some mishaps in our lives to remind us that we're not in total control of everything around us, but he is.

> *Rejoice in the Lord always. I will say it again: Rejoice!*
> —PHILIPPIANS 4:4

When I was about ten years old, my family went to a buffet-style restaurant. Going out to eat was a treat, so we would dress up. I put on a plaid wool skirt, a cream-colored blouse, and tights and then-fashionable wooden clogs.

As I wobbled into the restaurant, I probably looked like a monkey walking on stilts, but I felt grown-up and mature. That is, I did until I tried to walk across the polished, solid wood floor to our table. My feet flew up in front of me, and my backbone hit the floor with a thud.

It hurt all over, but I was more concerned about what I looked like than the throbbing in my back. People stopped what they were doing and stared. It was hands-down one of the most embarrassing moments in my life.

The older I get, the less I'm bothered by embarrassing moments. Making mistakes is a part of life, and I've learned to laugh at myself. There's a lot to be said about keeping a positive attitude—especially if you're a mom. Your attitude can quickly spread throughout the entire family. If Mama ain't happy, ain't nobody happy, right?

Psychologists have even discovered that moods are contagious. Like the flu, we pass along our attitudes to our families. In an article in *The Observer*, Shirley Wang stated, "The contagious quality of mood and emotion has been perhaps the most widely studied of all the different forms of contagion. People are extremely good at picking up on other people's emotions—both negative and positive—without consciously trying."

So if we stay lighthearted and laugh at life's mishaps, our kids will pick up on our positive attitude. In turn, they will pass that optimism along to others. Joy is a powerful ministry to anyone we come in contact with.

The Two Biggest Risks of Supper Swapping

Supper swapping adds a unique twist to your life, providing a new extended family of sorts—people who will be eating your cooking.

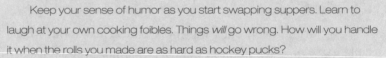

That's enough to make most of us stress out. I know if I bomb a meal and my family has to eat it, that's one thing. But to make a disaster of a meal for others? Well, that's another thing altogether. It's kind of like falling flat on your back in the middle of a crowded restaurant with everyone watching.

The two biggest risks I've found in supper swapping are meal-delivery mayhem and new-dish disasters.

Meal-Delivery Mayhem

When I first began supper swapping, Carla was in my group. Now, you have to know that Carla is one of those people who seems to have it all together. She is adorable, perky, energetic, and friendly. She has a soft-spoken voice and a quiet demeanor. She is always polite, warm, and sweet like a mocha latte on a cold winter's night. I thought I could never live up to her standards. That was, however, before I knew her well.

Carla and I had always been acquaintance friends. You know

one-gallon tub of soup spills during your meal delivery, are you expected to go home and make another batch, or can you gracefully bow out of that week's cooking day?

Accept others' cooking accidents. When your friend delivers dry meatloaf, pour a little ketchup on it and enjoy.

Always be loving. Always be kind. Always respect each other. And always laugh at life's curveballs.

the type—a friend of a friend, running into each other here and there, but never quite committing to a deeper friendship for one reason or another.

Then one day about seven years ago, my phone rang, and it was Carla. We chatted for a while and truly hit it off. Then she said something I will never forget: "Trish, I'd like to be closer friends with you. Do you have room in your life for one more girlfriend?"

Of course I had room for her! What I was afraid of was that she wouldn't like me—me, a mom with little patience who shouts at her kids on occasion and can even have a cluttered house. Though I was still a little intimidated, I said yes to her friendship and have been blessed by her ever since.

Amazingly enough, as sweet as Carla is, once I got to know her, I realized that she has just as many faults as I do. (Well, maybe not quite as many.) She has become one of my best friends, and I treasure her honesty and faith.

Carla, who started our supper-swapping group, had one of the biggest supper-swapping catastrophes on record. She was delivering her famous taco soup when the lid slipped off of her slow cooker. About a gallon of soup poured out all over her minivan. Poor thing. Just imagine the sticky mess and the spicy smell permeating the van. And we all know it's not easy to admit to hungry people relying on you that you have nothing to feed them. Moments like these are humbling to say the least. Carla ran home and cleaned out her van as best as she could, then graciously grabbed the soup she was saving for her own family to deliver to me.

At that time, I didn't realize what had happened. But a few days later, she told me the story, and we had a good laugh together. Understanding and empathy lightened what could have been a frustrating and embarrassing experience. We love and learn. We now all use those whale-of-a-pail ice-cream tubs to deliver soup. The lids snap on and spills are avoided.

New-Dish Disasters

Once, I made meatballs the size of tennis balls that were as dry as sand. Another time I made dumplings that turned out to be more like cardboard. Each time I delivered a disaster, my swapping buddies forgave me the faux pas, and we moved on, scratching that meal off our favorites list.

My supper-swapping friends would probably tell you those meals weren't really *that* bad, and they ended up eating them, but I was embarrassed at how they tasted. We all worry about our food, our cooking, and whether everyone likes it. Most of the time we all love what's delivered.

The best guard against new-dish disasters is to mix in only one or two new dishes a month, sticking to favorite recipes that work

Potluck Activity

THE BEST EVER!

Here is a great get-to-know-you activity to share with your supper-swapping girlfriends at your next meal-planning gathering.

Go around the table and take turns completing the following statements:

- The best pet I ever had was ...
- The best vacation I ever took was ...
- The best gift I ever received was ...
- The best song I ever heard was ...
- The best meal I ever had was ...

and everyone loves. We keep a running list of all the meals we prepare, and each time we plan for new meals, we star our group's favorites and cross off ones we won't be repeating—like cardboard dumplings.

Dear Lord, you give us the gift of joy and laughter. You want us to enjoy life. When life hands us a lemon, help us to discover the lemonade recipe you imprinted on our hearts. Sometimes we take things too seriously, we get upset too easily, and we forget that each day is a gift from you. Help us to enjoy every moment of every day, mishaps and all, always rejoicing and giving you praise. Amen.

Eleven

HONESTLY SPEAKING

Sharing Your Opinions without Hurting Feelings

To Tell the Truth

Honesty can be a challenge at times. Even for a girl like me. When I was in high school, I played on the basketball team. I loved sports, especially hoops. And I was pretty good. But I didn't quite fit in with the rest of the girls on the team. They were all friends on and off the court. My best friends included the

> *Let your conversation be always full of grace, seasoned with salt, so that you may know how to answer everyone.*
>
> COLOSSIANS 4:6

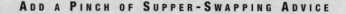

student council president, a cheerleader, and a few members of the honors math class. I straddled two worlds at once and didn't quite fit into either one as well as I would have liked.

My fellow honor students thought I was rough around the edges for being an athlete, and the cheerleaders didn't think I was popular enough. My teammates thought I was a goody two-shoes and began calling me Mary Poppins. It didn't really bother me because I knew they liked me. I was just different from them. So I settled for the nickname and found some honor in the fact that they thought I was sweet. It was enough for me to earn their respect on the court, which I did, and to accept who I was.

I probably am somewhat of a goody two-shoes, always trying to do what is right, sometimes ending up doing what is wrong. I am what my mom always called a "people pleaser," trying to make all those around me happy—or at least hoping they like me.

Over the years I have discovered that not everyone will like me, and I have settled for being what God intended me to be. I too mushy. Maybe next time, you could make your autumn soup with the crumbled bacon on top").

When someone asks you not to repeat a meal you've made for the group, don't take it as a personal attack. Realize that tastes vary, and not everyone likes what you do.

Meals that don't work well in your supper-swapping group can always be made on the weekends for your own family to enjoy.

Pray about your meal comments before making them. Be sure your honesty is clothed with kindness.

still struggle with that honesty thing, because I don't like hurting people's feelings.

I'm not the only people pleaser out there. You might be as much of a people pleaser as I am, trying hard to make everyone happy, running yourself ragged and trying not to let anyone down. I have met many moms who can't say no to a volunteer activity or turn down a committee position at church. Honesty is a tough thing to master, and I am still learning the finer points of telling the truth in love.

Meals That Miss

When I began supper swapping, it was difficult for me to be honest about the meals. I didn't want to say anything that might offend or hurt one of my friends. I wasn't alone. We were all walking the thin line of agreeableness and hardly ever said anything challenging. I didn't realize how bad it was until the chili incident.

When we had planned our meal calendar, I asked if everyone liked chili, and they all said yes. So when my cooking day arrived one week, I made scrumptious chili and served it with breadsticks. I delivered meals to Carla and Audrey, my group at the time, and assumed they and their families loved it.

Then about two months later, when we got together to plan the next set of meal calendars, I asked if they wanted me to make chili again. Carla said yes, but Audrey sat in silence.

I said, "Audrey, did your family like the chili? Audrey?"

She looked up at me like she was sitting on thumbtacks.

Then she said quietly, as softly as a whisper, "We don't eat chili."

"You don't eat chili?" I was dumbfounded.

"No, we don't like chili," she said.

"What did you do when I delivered the chili?"

"Well, my parents like chili, so I gave it to them for supper," Audrey said.

I wasn't sure whether to laugh or cry. Audrey looked like a deer caught in the headlights, and I felt bad for putting her on the spot.

Still I asked, "Why didn't you tell me that when we were planning our last meal calendars? I wouldn't have made it if I had known that your family doesn't eat chili."

"Well, Carla seemed to want it, and I didn't want to hurt your feelings," she said.

There it was. The honest truth. We were both so worried about hurting each other's feelings that we forgot why we were there in the first place—to simplify supper. So on the night I served chili to Audrey's family, she had to make a different meal on her own, which definitely didn't make her evening easier.

 # Potluck Activity

Here is a great get-to-know-you activity to share with your supper-swapping girlfriends at your next meal-planning gathering.

Give each person five small sheets of paper to write down answers to questions. You can answer each question either honestly, or you can try to fool your friends with a fake answer. Write the question number and your answer on each sheet of paper, but don't write your name.

Put all the completed papers in the center of the table. One by one, draw one out and read it aloud. Try to guess who wrote it and then guess if it is the truth or a lie.

1. How many men did you date before marrying your husband?

2. How old were you when you first learned the truth about Santa Claus?

3. How many mishaps happened at your wedding?

4. How many car accidents have you been in?

5. How many Oreos can you eat in one sitting?

For a moment, Carla, Audrey, and I sat in our corner booth at Applebee's and looked at each other. Then it began. I think Carla started to laugh, then I chuckled, and Audrey joined us. We sat there and laughed so loud, we almost made a scene.

We had talked about being honest with each other, but when push came to shove, we discarded honesty for the sake of avoiding hurt feelings. How silly was that! When we finally stopped laughing, we talked openly about how we could be more honest with each other, and that we had to be able to not take any meal discussion personally. We were closer friends after that night, and I never did make chili for the group again.

You have to express your likes and dislikes openly with your supper-swapping group. Find a way to be honest without sacrificing love, kindness, and respect. It can be done, and if you're up front about how meal discussions will be handled, you won't have a chili incident of your own!

Dear Lord, sometimes we don't realize how our words can hurt others. We speak too quickly, we speak too forcefully, and our words seem disrespectful, not honoring you at all. But we also know that we are called to be honest with each other. Sometimes it is difficult to find the balance between loving honesty and hurtful truths. Seal our lips with your grace so that our conversations are always full of love. Amen.

Twelve

THE GOOD-BYE GIRL

Moving Forward After Someone

Leaves Your Group

What Type of Friend Are You?

One of my favorite Christian speakers is Anita Renfroe. She is a
hoot and a holler. She speaks at women's conferences and is now
also speaking with Women of Faith (www.anitarenfroe.com).

She wrote a book called *The
Purse-Driven Life*, and I was blessed
to hear her speak at one of her
events this year. In between laughs
and chuckles, I discovered that I
have a purse-onality. I knew I was
kind of weird—have known that

> *In his heart a man
> plans his course, but
> the LORD determines
> his steps.*
>
> PROVERBS 16:9

since junior high. But when she described these purse-onalities, it was like she knew who I was. I'm sure I won't do her justice, but her explanation went something like this.

If you have girlfriends, look at the type of purse each is carrying. It will tell you exactly what type of friend she is. You can learn a lot about a gal by simply looking at her purse-onality.

If you have a girlfriend with a purse as big as a watermelon with candy, gum, tissues, and last year's Christmas list inside, keep her around. She's a keeper of all things, thrower-away of nothing. Should you ever find yourself in jail, she will be the friend with the nail file to help you break out.

If you have a girlfriend with a teeny, tiny little purse that is all clean, pretty, and perfect looking, keep her around. She's the shopper with money to spend. Should you wind up in jail someday, she will be the one to bail you out with the unlimited credit line on her charge card.

If you have a girlfriend who has had the same purse since 1995—all worn and tattered, beat up and shaggy—keep her around. She is loyal to the end. Should you wind up in jail someday, she will be the one marching in circles outside the jailhouse carrying protest signs proclaiming your innocence.

There were more purse-onalities, but I didn't hear any of them; I was too busy laughing and trying not to let out an obnoxious snort or something. I think I swallowed my breath mint. The lesson from the story is this: If you're blessed enough to hear Anita Renfroe in person, don't be sucking on a breath mint at the time—you might risk your life choking on it as you laugh so hard your belly hurts.

So what kind of purse-onalities do my supper-swapping girlfriends have?

Well, Teri bought a new purse this past year, and it's sort of a leather backpack thingamabob, very practical and yet beautiful. Teri's purse is well organized and efficient, holding everything she needs. Teri is the kind of friend who gives more than she gets and is always there when you need her most. She came over five years ago on the night I discovered I was having a miscarriage and just sat on the couch and cried with me. I think she's most definitely a keeper.

Nann is so much fun to be around. She and I have become even closer friends since we started swapping meals together. Her purse is probably the latest fashion, maybe with a sequin or two just for fun. Nann is the kind of friend who makes you laugh at yourself when you have food stuck between your teeth and takes you on the ride of your life, even if you're only going to the mall. I can truly let my hair down with Nann, laugh out loud, and maybe even let out a snort or two.

Kelly's purse is cute and clean, perky and bright. Kelly is all smiles, always kind, patient, and understanding. I find myself getting caught up in her joy. Her purse is probably full of breath mints and gum, tissues and shopping lists and whatever her friends need to borrow. She is the kind of friend who takes your hand, listens to your endless stories, and laughs when you laugh. Kelly is the kind of girlfriend you hope to have for a lifetime.

As for me, I have that same old purse that I have had for years. And though it is getting a bit ratty on the bottom, it is familiar and friendly. I am a loyal friend, one who doesn't like change. I would love it if the world would stay the same, and all my friends would remain by my side, and we could laugh and giggle and drink mocha lattes until our sides split.

But, unfortunately, life doesn't stand still. In fact, life seems to get more complex as it speeds along faster and faster. Like a rollercoaster ride racing down a hill without brakes, all I can do is sit back, try to relax, and hold on for dear life as life's twists and turns toss me about in my seat. Friends sometimes come and go in our lives and in our supper-swapping groups. I have had to learn to accept it, adapt to it, and grow in my faith because of it. That's just the way life is sometimes.

How to Say Good-bye to a Swapping Friend

Since it was Carla who initiated the supper-swapping idea, she pretty much ran the show. She kept us organized and encouraged. When Amy dropped out after only six months, I was disappointed but knew Carla and Audrey were still there to swap with me. The three of us were all committed to the idea, and we moved forward smoothly.

Right from the start, we all agreed we had to cherish our friendships above the swapping group, and that if and when any of us wanted to drop out, we had to be willing to let her go without making her feel guilty. But that sometimes is easier said than done.

As much as we don't like to admit it (especially publicly, like printed in a book for the entire world to read), there are some hurt feelings when a girlfriend leaves the group. As much as you know it isn't anything personal, a part of you feels rejected, as though maybe it was something you said or did. Maybe your cooking wasn't good enough. Maybe she got sick of seeing you so often, or maybe she just plain didn't want to be part of your group anymore.

Every time one of my friends dropped out of our group, it was like a breakup. We had become so much closer through supper swapping that losing the shared connection was difficult.

The loss of friendship. As much as I hate to admit it, there is a change in your friendship when you stop swapping with someone. It's not purposeful. It's not malicious. It's just a fact of life. When you're supper swapping with someone, there's a built-in framework for friendship. Like a puzzle with all the outside pieces in place, keeping the friendship going is as simple as adding another piece each week, snapping it into place as you talk on the phone or stop by to deliver your meals. You're connected to each other—a sort of sorority.

When a girlfriend drops out, it's more difficult to maintain the friendship at the same level. It's not out of spite, disappointment, or anger; there just aren't enough hours in the day.

I cherish my girlfriends, and each one brings a different personality into my life—a gift of love and laughter all her own. I don't want to lose any of them. I'm a loyal friend who hates change.

It was difficult for me when Amy left. We moved on without her, and though I don't see her as much as I would like to, our daughters are friends, and we try to get together when the girls have play dates as much as possible.

Then Audrey dropped out after swapping meals for about two years. That was much more devastating. Carla, Audrey, and I had swapped meals with just the three of us for almost a year until Teri joined, and we'd become a close-knit group by then. However, our husbands coach football together at the high school, and although I don't see Audrey as much as I would like to, I do try to call her. She's my friend who says it like it is, and I need her up-front honesty and confidence in my life.

The next domino to fall was Carla. She moved on after two and a half years. She was the one who always led the group, and she had been the girlfriend who originally brought supper swapping into my life. Carla's departure was probably the hardest for

ADD A PINCH OF SUPPER-SWAPPING ADVICE

Set guidelines. Agree to be honest, but never criticize; always appreciate.

Agree that when someone wants to drop out of the group, she should give one month's notice.

Agree that when someone leaves the group, she goes without letting any hurt feelings destroy the friendships.

When someone leaves your group, continue with the girlfriends who are left. Simply adjust your meal calendars for fewer meals and move forward prayerfully.

me to take. Though I understood her reasoning and respected her decision, I just couldn't imagine swapping suppers without her by my side. I thought it might be the end of supper swapping for me altogether.

But I knew God had a plan for our group, and I just had to be patient and seek his will. I may have lost Carla as a swapping partner, but I've kept her as one of my best friends. I can tell her anything, and she always listens and loves me no matter what. So I really haven't lost that relationship completely. Besides, I've learned that when people leave, God often introduces new and precious friendships into the group.

After two months of prayer, God brought Nann into our group and a wonderful new friendship into our lives. Teri, Nann, and I started swapping meals once again, and soon Kelly joined us.

You can also search for a replacement, but I recommend waiting a month and regrouping first. Pray about it before you add a new member.

Remember that the entire group must agree to invite someone in before you commit membership to a new swapper. You don't want your group to be cliquey, but you must make sure everyone will get along and work well together.

You can also take some time off from supper swapping if you like. Sometimes it's good to take a break and see where God is leading you.

Make sure to still include the girlfriends who dropped out of your supper-swapping group as a part of your life. Call them just to say hello. Plan a day at the park with your kids.

Forgiveness as spiritual medicine. I have no easy answer as to how to handle the disappointment and hurt feelings you may face when one of your girlfriends leaves your supper-swapping group. I am not sure there are any. What I do know is that God wants us to forgive "seventy-seven times" (Matt. 18:22) if we get hurt. That's our calling as Christians, and God will honor our willingness to forgive. We may plan our course, but God directs our steps, and we each must follow that lead. When a girlfriend chooses to leave the group, she is making the best decision for her family at that time, and you must honor that.

Forgiveness not only impacts the person being forgiven but also affects the health and well-being of the forgiver. An article by Dr. Christina Puchalski of Yale University School of Medicine discusses how our health is impacted by our willingness to forgive others—even small hurts: "The act of forgiveness can result in less anxiety and depression, better health outcomes, increased coping with stress, and increased closeness to God and others."

Life is full of disappointments, hurt feelings, frustrations, loved ones letting us down. Before you start swapping suppers, you must realize that swapping has a life cycle. For some families it's shorter than for others. Someone will leave your group at some point in time. Will you be ready and willing to let her go?

Each woman must make her own decision, and everyone else must respect that decision. Agree at the outset that you will cherish your friendships above the swapping group. Pray through any difficulties you encounter and honor one another's choices. God has a plan for your group. Seek his will, and everything else will fall into place.

Dear Lord, thank you for the gift of friendship, especially with our supper-swapping girlfriends. We know supper swapping doesn't last forever and that it will be a better fit for some of us than others. As we travel down the supper-swapping path, help us to understand when our friends leave our group. If we are the ones leaving, help us to do so lovingly and with compassion and kindness. If we are the ones being left, help us to continue to cherish our friendships. Amen.

# Potluck Activity

FINDERS KEEPERS

Here is a great get-to-know-you activity to share with your supper-swapping girlfriends at your next meal-planning gathering.

Give each person a few sheets of paper and a pencil. Spend some time talking about your friendships, how long you've known each other, how you became friends, and memories you share.

Then move away from the group and sit somewhere separately. Everyone then writes a letter to each of her friends in the group. Say why you like her, what her friendship means to you, and how she impacts your life.

After about twenty minutes, gather together again and hand out your letters. Decide whether you want to share them with the group or have each person take hers home to read privately.

Part Four

THE MINISTRY OF MEAL MAKING

Thirteen

MINISTERING THROUGH MEALS

How to Use Supper Swapping
as a Ministry

Ministering with Meals

When Riley was only six weeks old, I dropped her off at my mother-in-law's house so I could head to a PTO meeting at school. I had no idea we were on the verge of a nightmare.

Riley hadn't nursed very well that day, so I left a bottle in case she got hungry before I was back. She had

> Jesus said, "By this all men will know that you are my disciples, if you love one another."
>
> JOHN 13:35

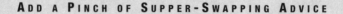

been fighting a cold, and breathing while nursing had become a challenge for her. As I sat at the meeting, something in me stirred. Call it motherly instinct. Call it intuition. Call it a gut feeling or a whisper from God. Whatever it was, I knew I needed to head home early. So I did.

When I walked into my mother-in-law's home thirty minutes later, Riley was still sleeping in her car seat. My mother-in-law said she had slept all the while, so she didn't take her out. I thanked her and headed for home, feeling uneasy about Riley's sleeping so much. She had hardly eaten all day, and mommy worries began to turn in my head.

When I got home, I decided to give her a bath to wake her up in hope that she might nurse before bed. By the time my husband arrived home from work, I was in a complete panic. Even the bath didn't wake her up. She was breathing very slowly, and she seemed unconscious.

We probably should have called an ambulance, but in the panic of the moment, we decided we could get her to the hospital faster. My in-laws came over to babysit, and we headed to the ER as fast as we could.

I sat in the backseat of the minivan, holding Riley in my lap. Every couple of minutes, her eyes would roll up in her head and her head would drop back. I would smack her cheek hard to bring her around. My heart was beating faster than I ever thought possible, and the tears were running down my face. I prayed feverishly that Riley might be okay, but in my mind, I pictured the worst. I thought we might lose our precious baby.

When we arrived at the ER, she was immediately put on

oxygen. After a long night and numerous tests, we discovered Riley had a severe case of RSV (respiratory syncytial virus), which can impede an infant's breathing. Over the next week, our days were filled with breathing treatments, oxygen tubes, and cold hospital-room chairs. I slept in a black leather recliner with Riley on my chest because she could breathe better sitting up than lying down. Mike spent his days traveling back and forth between the hospital and work, arranging for babysitting for our three older children, and coming to be with Riley and me.

After a few close calls, a spiked fever, and a lot of prayer, Riley finally began to get better. When we knew she would fully recover, we began counting our blessings and praising God.

I had been so caught up in our own tragedy that I hadn't given my supper-swapping group a second thought. When I arrived home after a week in the hospital, I was amazed to find a refriger-ator full of new meals and leftovers. My supper-swapping group at that time (Carla, Amy, and Audrey) had nourished my family when I wasn't able to. They kept right on delivering meals—even brought over extra food and sweet treats for my older kids. When I saw how full my fridge was, I felt like crying. It was such a bless-ing to come home from the hospital and have plenty of food to feed my family.

As I called each of them to thank them for all they had done, they each said, "Don't worry about delivering your meals for a while. Just settle in and get some rest. We'll keep bringing our meals over, and when you're rested and ready, you can jump back in." That was more than three years ago, and I still cherish the memories of my friends mothering my family for me, stepping in and loving them when I wasn't able to be there.

All three friends eventually dropped out of my supper-swapping group for various reasons. But each is still a cherished friend of mine, and I am blessed to have them in my life. Supper swapping is so much more than meal sharing. It's life sharing. My friends didn't just deliver meals to my family during my absence; they delivered love, hope, and faith.

The Five Faith Elements of Supper Swapping

You may wonder what Christianity has to do with swapping meals. The answer is that sharing food with your group has many faith aspects.

Supper swapping and fellowship. God calls us to live our lives in fellowship with one another, joining together in faith, family, and fun, glorifying God through it all. Romans 12:10 says, "Be devoted to one another in brotherly love. Honor one another above yourselves." Through swapping suppers, we join together in fellowship, devoting ourselves to helping one another out, and honoring each other. We build long-lasting friendships and glorify God through our fellowship.

Supper swapping and discipleship. Through forming a supper-swapping group, women can live out Christ's command to disciple one another, building stronger relationships within the body of Christ. God commands us in Matthew 28:19, "Therefore go and make disciples of all nations." Women disciple one another through friendships, strengthening their faith as they walk side by side with each other. They may also lead nonbelievers to faith in Christ through their friendships.

Supper swapping and servanthood. Supper swapping also gives women the ability to live a life of servanthood, challenging them to give generously as they serve others meals each week. Mark

10:45 says, "For even the Son of Man did not come to be served, but to serve, and to give his life as a ransom for many."

Sometimes, as a wife and a mom, I feel overwhelmed. My life seems to revolve around the needs of my husband and my children. I'm not sure I want to serve anyone else, not sure there's anything left for me to give.

But the amazing thing is that the more we give, the more God provides for us. You can't out-give God. As you reach out to other moms, inviting them to share their burdens with you and helping them nourish their families through supper swapping, you'll be amazed at how much God gives you in return!

Supper swapping and stewardship. God blesses us daily with our health, money, possessions, and abilities. It's a huge responsibility to honor God with what we're given. The first step is to realize that nothing belongs to us; everything belongs to God. We're like the servants in the parable of the talents, the ones God has entrusted with gifts: "His master replied, 'Well done, good and faithful servant! You have been faithful with a few things; I will put you in charge of many things. Come and share your master's happiness!'" (Matt. 25:21).

Through supper swapping, families are more equipped to budget their grocery expenditures, eat out less, and waste less money in the frenzy to feed themselves. Good stewardship frees up their resources so they can support their church, give generously to those in need, and live within their means. Their time is also spent more frugally, with less time needed for cooking supper, allowing for more family time in the evenings.

Supper swapping and evangelism. Supper swapping opens the door for friendships, which open the door for relationship evangelism, a strong force for leading a lost world to Christ. In Philippians 2:15–16, God calls us to "shine like stars in the universe as you hold out the word of life," and the best way to shine is to show others we care. But no one will see us shine or care that we are shining unless they know us. It's like that old adage, "People don't care what you know until they know that you care."

In *Executable Outlines*, Mark Copeland discusses the two primary ways Christians can evangelize the lost world. The first is the message of the gospel itself, the saving grace of faith in Christ. The second is the manifestation of the gospel message in the life of the Christian, which we should be striving toward in all we do.

But reaching a lost world for Christ isn't easy. Copeland discusses other studies that have shown that the most effective evangelism tool is building relationships with nonbelievers and inviting them into our lives and into our faith. A survey by the Institute for American Church Growth asked more than ten thousand people why they came to church and faith in Christ. Amazingly, an overwhelming 79 percent responded that they came because "a friend or relative invited me." That's the power of relationship evangelism, which you can discover through the most unlikely of means—supper swapping!

Dear Lord, thank you for leading us in our faith, for touching our hearts and opening our eyes to the truth of salvation in Jesus. We know we are your disciples. We ask you to help us show our faith by what we say and do. Help us to love one another—our friends and our enemies—so that when others see us, they see a reflection of you. Please help us to minister to others through our supper-swapping group, in little and big ways. Amen.

Potluck Activity

CARD SHARK!

Here is a great get-to-know-you activity to share with your supper-swapping girlfriends at your next meal-planning gathering.

Shuffle a deck of cards; give each person three cards turned face down on the table in front of them. One at a time, the person turns over a card over to reveal the number or the face card. She must provide an answer to the following questions as many times as the number on the card. For example, if she reveals a three (the suit doesn't matter), then she must list three items; a nine of any suit, list nine items; aces and face cards are worth ten.

As you turn over a card, answer the following:

Card No. 1   Names of restaurants you like

Card No. 2   Places you have vacationed in your life

Card No. 3   Places your husband has taken you on a date

GROWING A GARDEN OF FRIENDS

Building Deeper Friendships through Supper Swapping

A Garden of Friendships, a Lifetime of Growth

Some friendships start when we are young—little girls with big dreams searching the playground for someone like you. Someone to giggle with at the slightest joke or stay up with until dawn talking about whatever little girls talk about. Someone to weep with us

> *A friend loves at all times.*
> PROVERBS 17:17

when our heart is broken and jump for joy when we are blessed. We're searching for a friend.

Often, when little-girl friendships come into our lives, we are too immature to appreciate what we have when we have it. I know I never did. If we are one of the lucky ones, we hold on to those childhood friendships as we grow up. Year after year, we tend to that friendship, nourish its roots, and watch it blossom like a flower. But most of the time, we let go of our schoolgirl friend-ships somewhere around the time we set off for college, marriage, motherhood, or a career.

Like most moms, many of my little-girl friendships were left behind when life became busy. It's not that I wanted to let them go, but little by little, we simply grew apart. The funny thing is, as I grew up, I carried all the same hopes and dreams from my youth with me into adulthood. I guess I'm wrapped up in pigtails and pixies on the inside even though I'm perms and pumps on the outside.

My best friend in the whole world from sixth grade through college was Lisa McClain. She and I went through it all together. She even tried out for the junior high basketball team, just so we could be together, even though she couldn't sink a shot if her life depended on it. We were there for our first crushes, our first dates, school dances, and too many Friday-night sleepovers to count. We would sit up all night laughing and talking. We were there when our parents got divorced and our dads became strangers. We went to separate colleges but were bridesmaids in each other's weddings. Soon after, life seemed to get in the way of our friendship.

I hold a special place in my heart for Lisa. I was able to visit her last Christmas for the first time in almost a decade. Funny thing, when I walked into her home, it was like stepping back into my youth. She was the same little girl with blonde hair, blue eyes, and that killer smile I remembered. We talked for hours on end as our children played. When it was time for me to leave, my heart felt slightly broken all over again because I knew we wouldn't see each other for a long while.

But God is so good, and he has blessed me with some of the best grown-up friends anyone could ask for, amazing women who remind me to laugh when I trip over my feet or my words. Friends who like me for who I am, wipe my tears, and laugh at all of my dumb jokes. I am able to survive the daily demands of motherhood because they are right beside me, cheering me on.

The Importance of Friendships for Women

Women need to communicate. We need to share our hearts, our feelings, and our thoughts with others. The problem is that sometimes our husbands don't need (or want) to listen to all of that. It's not their fault—they're just made differently than women (you know, from Mars and all that). God made women unique, and we have different needs than men do. For women, having strong friendships with other women is an important part of their lives.

In an article from *Psychology Today* titled "Tend and Befriend," Nancy Dess discusses a landmark UCLA study that found friendship between women is different from friendship between men. In times of stress, men fight or flee. They either get angry and fight it out or leave the situation. In times of stress, women tend and befriend. They nurture their children with hugs and kisses, and turn to their girlfriends by "talking on the phone or doing lunch."

As women tend and befriend, certain hormones are released into their system making them feel better. In fact, because of this tend-and-befriend action, having close girlfriends reduces your stress levels and could help you live longer and better. Another study went even further and proved that "women with the most friends over a nine year period cut their risk of death by 60 percent" (Women and Friendships).

But as busy moms, when life gets in the way and our schedules get crazy, the first thing we let go of is our friendships. We don't prioritize our own needs above those of our families. That's motherhood.

Building Friendships through Supper Swapping

One of the greatest gifts of supper swapping is the framework for friendship that is automatically built in. Like a puzzle piece that clicks perfectly into place and snaps into the rest of the picture, supper swapping snaps friendship into my life with little effort and great reward.

Supper swapping has helped me plant a garden of girlfriends and tend to those relationships, nurturing them and watching them blossom like a colorful flower garden. It all begins with a simple seed you plant—an invitation to swap suppers. If you tend it right, that seed can grow into an incredible friendship that blesses your life more than you ever imagined. Whether your supper-swapping group lasts six months or six years, no matter who comes and goes, the friendships you establish and nurture can bless you for a lifetime.

We've done a variety of things to nurture our friendships over the years, from having a girls' night out to a date night. It doesn't matter what you do as long as you take time to get together, get to know each other, and nurture your friendships.

Plant Seeds of Friendship

To nourish your garden of friendships, spend time together outside of swapping meals. Here are a few fun ideas.

Girls' night out. The women in our group try to get together once every few months for late-night appetizers and iced tea at a local Applebee's. Because it's open until midnight, we don't meet until 9:00 p.m., after we've eaten supper with our family, helped our kids with their homework, and tucked them into bed. Our husbands are home, eliminating the need for a babysitter, so we can get together for a guilt-free girls' night out.

We also plan some fun into our meal-planning get-togethers. We meet once every three months and take turns hosting the event. The hostess makes a delightful sweet treat to share, and as we sip coffee and tea, we spend as much time chatting about life as we do planning our meals.

Date night. We try to plan one or two date nights with our husbands as a group. This is a little more involved since we all have to arrange for babysitting. All eight adults go out for a nice dinner and sometimes return to one of our homes for dessert and a few board games. This gives our husbands a chance to get to know each other, and we all become closer friends.

Family fun night. We schedule one or two family nights yearly when we all get together—moms, dads, and kids (quite a crew!). One year, we had a campfire and weenie roast at our family farm and spent the evening watching the sunset over the hills as we enjoyed the quietness of the countryside and way too many s'mores.

Tending to Your Friendship Garden

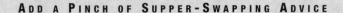

I finally made the break. I decided not to plant a vegetable garden this spring. It was the first time in more than a decade that I didn't plow the earth in my little plot and toss in seeds on a whim and a prayer. Life had been getting busier and busier, and I knew that if I did plant a vegetable garden, all I would probably grow were weeds and guilt—weeds because I knew I wouldn't have enough time to tend to my garden, and guilt because every time I

Plan a date night once or twice a year. This is when your husbands get to come along so they can build friendships with the other men in the group. It can be as simple as going out to dinner or over to someone's house for pizza.

Call a group member once a week or so. There's nothing sweeter than getting a phone call from a girlfriend for no other reason than "just because."

Offer to babysit for one of your supper-swapping girlfriends once in a while. We trade babysitting on occasion and always help out when one of us is in a pinch.

Ask how you can pray for each other's family. Include a short prayer or Bible verse on your meal calendars, something you can all read throughout the month and be in unison in your prayers.

looked out my front window at my weed-embedded garden I would feel guilty for letting it get so bad.

So this year, no garden.

Gardens are a lot of work. You can't just plant a seed, walk away, and expect to harvest a decent crop. Just look at my flower beds. I planted some bright pink and orange perennials this spring but was so busy this summer that I didn't weed much at all. The weeds started growing, and soon they overtook the flowers. It got to the point where the thought of trying to weed those beds was so overwhelming that I gave up. I threw my hands in the air and decided my new gardening technique was *gardening by survival of the fittest.* Whatever grew and survived could stay and decorate our yard.

That may be acceptable for gardening, but for friendships, the weeds can actually choke out the love if you don't pull them when they're still small. There are five main ways you can harvest a garden of friends: plant the seed, pour out forgiveness, pray through the weeds, prune bad feelings, and play in the garden.

Plant the seed. For your friendship garden to thrive you need to plant it in fertile soil, tend and weed it, and allow your friendships to grow roots. How many friends do you have who truly know you, who have seen you first thing in the morning—in your pajamas, with messy hair and smelly breath? How many of your friends know your mommy struggles and your daily challenges?

When we first began supper swapping, I knew exactly what time the meals were being delivered each day. I would make sure I'd had my shower, was dressed, hair done, and usually had makeup on when my friends arrived. I might even light a few candles for ambiance. The kitchen was clean, and there were no toys in the living room. But that was a lot of work. I've discovered that one of the greatest gifts we can give our girlfriends is to have them over and *not* clean up the house. When they see our house as it truly is, mess and all, they feel right at home. They're also comforted to know they don't have to feel uncomfortable when we come over to their cluttered houses. Let's face it—life is stressful enough without trying to always look good for your girlfriends.

I think supper swapping gives you the opportunity to become more vulnerable with your girlfriends. As time goes on, each of you will find it easier to be more open about life's challenges and will end up revealing your heart and accepting more than just one another's messy houses. You will end up even sharing your messy lives, kids, thoughts, feelings, and faith as well. In that sense, your relationship roots grow deeper and are more meaningful, and you are able to build stronger friendships than you ever thought possible!

Pour out forgiveness. Every garden needs water to grow, and your garden of girlfriends needs to be watered by the refreshing grace of forgiveness. A friend hurts our feelings, says something she didn't mean, or unintentionally offends us or ones we love. It happens—it's a fact of life. It will most certainly be experienced by your supper-swapping group. How you handle these circumstances will define what kind of a friend you are.

Life is too short to live without the water of forgiveness. Friends are too precious to let wither on the vine of anger. Your friendships will last only if you're willing to wash them in the same grace of forgiveness God has blessed us with. Your supper-swapping friendships will blossom only if they're watered.

Pray through the weeds. Realize there will be times when your feelings are hurt, or you feel group members have intruded on your life, judged you, or not included you in an event. We're not perfect beings, and we're not perfect friends. When you feel a weed of discontent creeping into your garden, pray about it. Ask the group to pray with you.

Prune bad feelings. Most of my friends will tell you that they rarely have to guess what I am thinking. I tell them. I am a woman of many words, what some might call a big mouth. But I am open and honest, but tenderhearted as well. That's why when someone hurts my feelings I usually keep it to myself. That sounds good in theory, except that I let those hurt feelings become bad feelings. Those bad feelings fester and rot up my heart like a compost pile, and I can sometimes end up getting angry.

Women are emotional beings; we feel everything, good and bad. But if we let hurt feelings become angry emotions, we can hurt or lose friendships. The best thing to do when someone hurts your feelings is to be honest and tell her. Chances are, she didn't realize she had hurt you, and you can talk it over and work it out. It is so much better to prune bad feelings when they are small than to let them grow and spread until they are growing out of control. Pruning bad feelings with your friends will allow you to grow life-long friendships based on trust and honesty.

Play in the garden. God created laughter; God gave us the gift of joy. Life is about more than just getting work done. It's about

 Potluck Activity

A T R E A S U R E   H U N T

Here is a great get-to-know-you activity to share with your supper-swapping girlfriends at your next meal-planning gathering.

Go to the dollar store and buy one gift for each of your supper-swapping girlfriends. Wrap your treasures and, at your next meal-planning meeting, exchange gifts. Discuss why you chose each gift and share one story of your friendship with the group—maybe something funny that happened when you were together, a trip you took together, or a silly movie you once saw.

enjoying every moment we have this side of heaven. Sometimes we take life too seriously and forget to find joy in our mundane tasks or laughter in our everyday mishaps. Friendships blossom when we laugh with and enjoy each other. Your supper-swapping group will bloom and grow a garden of friendships if you remember to take the time to laugh.

Whatever comes your way, look for the upside. Though our lives may get bumpy at times, God is in control. He has a plan for you, and part of that plan is to be joyful despite life's circumstances. Draw on your supper-swapping friends to help you maintain that joy.

Dear Lord, we praise you for the gift of friendship, for friends who seem to understand our needs, laugh at our jokes, see us for who we are, accept our imperfections, and love us anyway. As we share the burdens and blessings of nourishing our families, help us to draw closer to one another in friendship and closer to you in faith. Amen.

.Fifteen.

SUPPER-SWAPPING INSPIRATION

Scriptures, Sayings, and Quotes to Swap Along with Your Meals

As you swap suppers, don't forget to swap love, friendship, encouragement, and faith as well. Here are some Bible verses and phrases you can jot down on your meal calendars or cooking instructions to help you do just that.

Blessings

Blessings crown the head of the righteous. (Prov. 10:6)
Nothing blessed my life more than a great epidural.
Blessings are sometimes disguised as children.
Little blessings are like tiny grains of sugar that sweeten your day.

You know you're a mom when your blessings come in whispers and hugs.

Blessings sometimes look like disappointments, until you look closer.

Begin each day counting your blessings, and see how they add up.

Kids are the blessings that greet me in the morning. Otherwise, I would sleep in.

Blessings come in three sizes: tall, grande, and venti.

Children

Having a child is like letting your heart grow legs.

Teach a child to love and you have blessed the world.

Kids are full of endless questions and love is the answer to them all.

Nothing is sweeter than a sticky peanut-butter kiss from your toddler—except for the one that is followed by a chocolate kiss.

Kids think the world is their napkin.

The true secret to life is why kids pick their nose then lick their finger.

Make your child smile: Let him eat cookies for breakfast.

A spoon full of sugar does make the medicine taste better.

Comfort

As a mother comforts her child, so will I comfort you. (Isa. 66:13)

Comfort comes in flavors: mocha or caramel latte.

Cast your cares on the LORD and he will sustain you. (Ps. 55:22)

Velcro hugs are the best comfort ever invented.

Jesus wept. (John 11:35)

Comfort your child with hot cocoa and tender love.

"Surely I am with you always, to the very end of the age." (Matt. 28:20)

Comfort is a comfy pair of sweatpants and a fuzzy pair of slippers.

Pain comes from without—comfort comes from within.

Courage

I can do everything through him who gives me strength. (Phil. 4:13)

Courage is getting out of bed each morning.

"Do not let your hearts be troubled. Trust in God; trust also in me." (John 14:1)

Courage is not something you do; it is the way you live.

Courage is becoming a mom.

The LORD is my light and my salvation—whom shall I fear? (Ps. 27:1)

Courage is being afraid and moving forward anyway.

The LORD is the stronghold of my life—of whom shall I be afraid? (Ps. 27:1)

True courage is taking your toddler to the grocery store without a bag of M&M's to feed him.

Courage is getting pregnant again knowing that your last epidural failed.

Encouragement

Chocolate is the only encouragement I need.

Friends encourage each other by just being there.

Friends let friends sing off key, and join in anyway.

You are a shield around me, O LORD; you bestow glory on me and lift up my head. (Ps. 3:3)

Smile at a stranger and pass hope around.

There is faith in friendship, power in prayer, and energy in encouragement.

I lift up my eyes to the hills—where does my help come from? My help comes from the LORD, the Maker of heaven and earth. (Ps. 121:1–2)

Encouragement is elastic—it always bounces back at you.

Faith

Faithful living is getting out of bed even when you're out of Pop-Tarts.

Faith is the seed that is planted in times of joy and harvested in times of sorrow.

Have faith in the LORD your God and you will be upheld. (2 Chron. 20:20)

Faith is looking in the mirror and seeing what others see.

The LORD is good and his love endures forever; his faithfulness continues through all generations. (Ps. 100:5)

Being faithful is as simple as saying yes to God.

Faith may begin as a spark in the night, but ends as a fire in the soul.

Faith is pulling out your before-kid jeans and trying to squeeze into them.

Family

In-laws are like foreigners. Try to speak their language for a change.

A strong family is like a baseball team. You just have to know who the Coach is.

Family traditions are the glue that holds us together.

Above all, love each other deeply, because love covers over a multitude of sins. (1 Peter 4:8)

We are all God's children. Some of us just forget we have siblings.

The family that shares one bathroom is truly close knit.

He who finds a wife finds what is good and receives favor from the LORD. (Prov. 18:22)

The key to loving your family is first accepting that you aren't perfect.

Forgiveness

You are forgiving and good, O LORD, abounding in love to all who call to you. (Ps. 86:5)

Forgiveness is the water that soothes the soul.

The sunshine warms your skin, but only forgiveness warms your heart.

Forgiveness is the sweetest fruit you could taste.

Be kind and compassionate to one another, forgiving each other, just as in Christ God forgave you. (Eph. 4:32)

Forgiveness means saying you're sorry even when you were right.

Marriage is made stronger by forgiveness.

Friendship only lasts when watered with forgiveness and grace.

Mistakes might happen by accident. But only forgiveness is given on purpose.

Forgiveness is like a cool autumn breeze that blows through your soul.

Friendship

There is a friend who sticks closer than a brother. (Prov. 18:24)

True friends love you, even without your makeup on.

He who walks with the wise grows wise. (Prov. 13:20)

Friends guard each other's hopes and dreams as if they were their own.

Give your girlfriend a gift—don't clean up before she comes over. She'll feel right at home.

Hope that is shared with a friend can inspire a dream.

You are the God who sees me. (Gen. 16:13)

If you want to have a friend, be a friend first.

A true friend cries with you, laughs with you, and sits with you when words won't help.

Nothing tastes better than a mocha latte shared with a friend.

Gifts

Give the gift of friendship. It can always be returned.

Unwrapped gifts are a hidden treasure.

[God] gives strength to the weary and increases the power of the weak. (Isa. 40:29)

Smiling at someone is like giving them hope.

Give more than you receive, and you'll get more than you gave.

Share your gifts with the world and watch what God can do.

Nothing says "I love you" more than noodle hearts or turkey handprints.

The gift of morning always comes too early.

Grace

But [the Lord] said to me, "My grace is sufficient for you, for my power is made perfect in weakness." (2 Cor. 12:9)

Grace is like getting something for free.

God's grace turns a mountain into an ant hill.

May God be gracious to us and bless us and make his face shine upon us. (Ps. 67:1)

Graceful living is serving love as a main dish every day.

Grace is staying awake through bedtime prayers that last longer than a light opera.

If you can't let go of your anger, give it to God. His grace is sufficient.

Grace is being able to see the world through others' eyes.

Home

"In my Father's house are many rooms; if it were not so, I would have told you. I am going there to prepare a place for you." (John 14:2)

Home is where you can walk around barefoot.

Home is where you're loved most.

Home is a place we long for, somewhere we are loved.

A house is built with wood and brick, but a home is built on love.

You know you are home when you can be yourself.

You give your kids a home when you give them your heart.

Hope

Find rest, O my soul, in God alone; my hope comes from him. (Ps. 62:5)

Having hope is getting up in the morning after being up with a newborn at night.

No one whose hope is in you will ever be put to shame. (Ps. 25:3)

Faith rests in the sunset, but hope rises with the sun.

My hope lies in the coffeepot working every morning.

Hope for tomorrow begins with faith for today.

Joy

In him our hearts rejoice, for we trust in his holy name. (Ps. 33:21)

Where your treasure is, there your heart will be also. (Matt. 6:21)

Joy is having Lucky Charms in the pantry.

Be joyful in all you do. Make others wonder why.

Kids know how to be joyful—follow their lead.

When you don't feel joyful, just fake it. Soon you will feel it.

Rejoice and be glad, because great is your reward in heaven. (Matt. 5:12)

Love

Your love, O LORD, reaches to the heavens, your faithfulness to the skies. (Ps. 36:5)

Kiss your husband every morning. He might just wonder what you're up to.

I trust in your unfailing love; my heart rejoices in your salvation. (Ps. 13:5)

Never forget to treat your husband like he's your sweetheart.

God is love. Whoever lives in love lives in God, and God in him. (1 John 4:16)

True love overcomes trials by holding fast to yesterday.

Beloved, let us love one another: for love is of God; and every one that loveth is born of God, and knoweth God. He that loveth not knoweth not God; for God is love. (1 John 4:7–8 KJV)

I never knew love until I held my child's hand.

Love from a child is as sweet as honey, and sometimes as sticky, too.

Miracles

Miracles are everyday occurrences that surprise us, but not God.

It's a miracle when I wake up before the alarm clock goes off.

Don't underestimate the power of ordinary miracles.

Miracles are prayers disguised as blessings.

Ordinary days are miracles from heaven.

Motherhood

If you know who Arthur, Ord, and Elmo are, you must be a mom.

Motherhood is the most humbling job you will ever have.

If having Frosted Flakes in your pantry makes for a glorious morning, you must be a mom.

If you can change a diaper faster than a rodeo cowboy can rope a calf, you must be a mom.

If you have stretch marks in places you didn't know could stretch, you must be a mom.

Patience

A patient man has great understanding. (Prov. 14:29)

Patience is wanting tomorrow but living for today.

Wait for the LORD, and he will deliver you. (Prov. 20:22)

Patience is waiting for your epidural to kick in.

I am not a patient person. Even the microwave takes too long.

My kids have taught me to be more patient. I can wait for them to grow up.

Praise

Make a joyful noise unto the LORD. (Ps. 100:1 KJV)

Compliments and praise should be given out freely.

From the lips of children and infants you have ordained praise, [O Lord]. (Ps. 8:2)

Praise a child and feed his or her soul.

Words of praise are like songs that are sung from heart to heart.

Enter his gates with thanksgiving and his courts with praise. (Ps. 100:4)

Praise your husband daily and see what a treasure he is.

Praise is too often forgotten, most often what is needed.

Part Five

GARNISHES FOR YOUR SUPPER-SWAPPING KITCHEN

Sixteen

Q&As

Answers to All Your Supper-Swapping

Questions

Q. What is supper swapping?

A. Supper swapping is friends helping friends, moms helping moms. It's a proven method of simplifying your dinner preparation, reducing your cooking time by 80 percent, and saving you time, money, and stress. You gather a few friends who are struggling, just like you, with that four-thirty-and-nothing's-in-the-oven panic and form a supper-swapping group.

Q. How does supper swapping work?

A. You cook one day a week, making five identical meals. You keep one for your family and deliver the others to the four families in your group. The rest of the week, group members deliver supper to you. The best part? The rest of the week your kitchen counters stay clean.

> The joy of the LORD is your strength.
>
> NEHEMIAH 8:10

Q. Is supper swapping the same thing as once-a-month cooking?

A. Not really. Both once-a-month cooking and supper swapping are meal-simplification methods, but they meet those needs in different ways.

With once-a-month cooking, you spend an entire day preparing a variety of meals, enough to cover your family suppers for an entire month. Then you put all those meals in freezer-safe containers and store them in the freezer. There are methods of combining the meal-simplification technique of once-a-month cooking with the friendship of supper swapping by forming a group. Instead of swapping fresh meals daily, you each prepare meals in bulk that can be frozen and then swap those frozen meals once a month. For more information on this method, see *Cooking Among Friends* by Mary Tennant and Becki Visser or *Supper Swapping* by Susan Thacker.

Q. Do we have to swap meals daily, or can we swap meals weekly or monthly?

A. You set up your supper-swapping group to swap meals whenever you want to. That's the benefit of supper swapping: It can be tailored to meet the needs and schedules of the families involved.

Q. Does supper swapping work only for stay-at-home moms?

A. Supper swapping works for any family dynamic, from families with stay-at-home moms to families with working moms; even single-parent families and retired grandparents can simplify their dinnertime needs by swapping suppers with neighbors and friends. All you need to do is set up your group to meet your needs and fit your schedule. If daily meal swapping doesn't work well for your group because you'll be at work, your group could meet at someone's house on Sunday evenings and swap all your meals at once.

Supper swapping is also a great way for seniors to build a stronger sense of community and deeper friendships. Retired adults may even decide to eat together daily, rotating the hosting responsibility through the group.

Q. How do I find friends or neighbors who might want to swap suppers with me?

A. The first thing you should do is to pray about this decision. There probably are many families in your own neighborhood or friends you already have who are struggling with their own dinnertime dilemmas. Seek God's guidance about whom to approach about trying to form a supper-swapping group. When you do approach them, ask them to read this book so they'll have a good idea of how the whole thing works. Then, plan an informal get-together to discuss the possibilities.

Q. What if no one wants to try supper swapping?

A. Don't get discouraged. It is a new idea that may seem strange to some at first. Don't push the concept on others. Maybe suggest they try it for a one-month trial period to see if they like it, after which they can leave the group. People are usually more likely to try supper swapping when they know they aren't locked in for life, or that you won't be angry with them if they choose to leave the group. Even if you have only one friend willing to give it a try, you'll find swapping one or two meals a week simplifies your life. Others will see how smoothly it's going, and they'll ask how they can join.

Q. What if my kids are picky eaters?

A. I have two picky eaters in my family, and they seem more excited about eating what other moms make for supper than what I make. Go figure. I think it's that grass-is-always-greener thing.

   Something you can do to make it easier is for your supper-swapping group to incorporate a kid-friendly family favorite at least once or twice a week—like baked macaroni and cheese, tacos, or spaghetti. You might also include your kids in the planning process by asking them what meals they would like to see on the meal-planning calendar. I guarantee they'll eat the meals they request!

Q. Why is eating supper together as a family so important?

A. Only 50 percent of American families today are eating supper together regularly, mainly because we're all just too busy to sit down for a family meal. Yet, research has proven time and again that supper is the glue that holds a family together. Eating dinner together teaches your children that they're a priority in your life, opens the door for communication between parents and children, encourages healthy eating habits, and helps prevent eating disorders, obesity, and poor choices later in life (especially teenage smoking, drinking, and drug abuse). It also gives you an opportunity to pass on your faith to your children as you say a family prayer or read a devotion while at the table.

Q. How do I get started swapping suppers?

A. First, read *The Great American Supper Swap*. Then ask a few friends or neighbors if they're interested in swapping suppers with you. Plan an informal gathering to discuss the possibilities and decide how your swapping group will work. It's that simple!

Q. What if my husband is reluctant to try supper swapping?

A. First of all, even though our husbands may not be doing the cooking, they *are* doing the eating, so supper swapping will impact them almost as much as it impacts us. This must be a family decision—one everyone is comfortable with. If you've discussed supper swapping with your husband, and he seems reluctant to try it, pray about it and see where God leads. Then ask your husband to try it for one month and agree to leave the group after that month if he still isn't convinced. That usually works. That and telling him he will have a hot, fresh supper every night of the week!

Q. How long will it take me to make the meals on my cooking day?

A. I usually spend one to two hours preparing my meals on my cooking day. Some meals are easy to assemble, like Meatballs and Sausage. Others take longer. The key is to pick meals to swap that aren't difficult to prepare. Keep it simple.

Q. How long will meal delivery take?

A. I live in a very rural area of Ohio. Everyone in my group lives within ten miles of me, but definitely not next door. My meal delivery takes about a half hour from start to finish. But some supper swappers are neighbors, living next door or down the street, reducing meal delivery time significantly. The key is including families that live close to you so meal delivery isn't an added burden.

Q. How do you schedule meal deliveries when our families have such diverse and demanding schedules?

A. One of the most powerful tools of supper swapping is its flexibility. You can tailor delivery time to fit each family's schedule. Meals don't need to be delivered at the same time every day. Nann delivers her meal Monday evening at 5:00 p.m. Teri delivers hers Tuesdays at noon. Kelly and I alternate Wednesday delivery, so we drive only twice a month and each delivers sometime in the afternoon.

To give you greater flexibility with meal delivery, you can share your garage-door codes, leave a key somewhere, or leave a cooler with ice on your porch for the meal. It's up to you and what you're all comfortable with.

Q. What if someone drops out of the group?

A. It's always difficult when someone decides to leave your group. But you must cherish the friendship above the group and let the departing group member leave guilt-free. We usually ask for the courtesy of one month's notice prior to leaving the group. The best thing to do is to continue to swap suppers with the group members who are left and pray about seeking a new person to join you. Don't get discouraged. You can swap suppers with as few as two friends, still simplifying dinnertime.

Q. What if I can find only one friend who is interested in swapping suppers?

A. My best advice is to go ahead and get swapping! It's actually a great way to start. Two people can swap one or two meals each week. It still saves you time and money. You could make two meals on Monday, delivering one to your friend. Eat leftovers on Tuesday. Then Wednesday, she could make two meals, delivering one to you with enough leftovers for Thursday. Or you could each make two main dishes that use similar ingredients, simplifying the preparation process. You could make two pans of spaghetti and meatloaf on Monday, delivering one of each to your friend, which covers supper Monday and Tuesday. Then on Wednesday, she could make chicken pot pies and chicken noodle soup and deliver those to you for Wednesday and Thursday. Voilà, a week's worth of meals.

Q. I'm not an expert cook. What if the other families don't like my cooking?

A. Supper swapping isn't about gourmet cooking. If your own family enjoys your cooking, chances are other families will as well. When you begin swapping suppers, pick recipes that your family loves, ones that are easy to make. One of our favorite meals is Nann's taco bar with seasoned beef, soft and hard taco shells, and all the fixings to make our own tacos. How simple is that?

Q. What if someone joins our group, and we discover we don't like her food?

A. That's a tough question. My best advice is not to get into this situation in the first place. You should form your supper-swapping group with people whose food you've already tasted, maybe at a covered-dish church dinner or at a picnic. If you find yourself in that situation, remember to be kind and loving. Not liking the food probably has more to do with the recipes she's making rather than her skill level. You could request different recipes.

Q. How can I save money swapping suppers?

A. First of all, plan your meals three months at a time. Then, make a list of all the meals you're making and their ingredients. Keep that list in your purse. When you go grocery shopping, look it over and see what's on sale. Any ingredients that you can store or freeze can be bought ahead of time, saving you money. You can also buy your ingredients in bulk, saving additional money. Overall, you'll waste less food since you're going to the grocery store with a plan. Most families save at least fifty to eighty dollars a month swapping suppers.

Q. How do we make sure we're all spending the same amount on our meals?

A. This isn't really necessary and would be an added burden to track. If you all agree at the outset to a range of meal costs, that's good enough. Then you can alternate more-expensive meals with less-expensive ones each month, staying within your family budget. Most supper-swapping families spend between twenty and sixty dollars per week on their meals.

Q. What if we have food allergies in our family?

A. When you form your group, you need to make a list of all the food allergies and food dislikes family members have. You could just leave those ingredients out of the meals. Mike doesn't like mushrooms, so when Kelly makes beef stroganoff, she keeps the mushrooms in a separate disposable storage container so whoever likes them can add them at suppertime.

Q. I love to cook. I'm wondering if I'll miss fixing dinner every night for my family.

A. Supper swapping isn't about hating to cook. It's about simplifying your life. You'll still have plenty of time to spend cooking with and for your own family on weekends, and you might discover that you enjoy cooking even more when the pressure to cook every night is off.

Q. Will I need any special equipment, pots, pans, or containers?

A. We use 9x13-inch glass oven-safe baking dishes with snap-on lids and semidisposable storage containers just to keep it simple. But you can use pans you already own. Just make sure you don't swap meals in pans or containers that you want to get back. What you contribute to the swapping group will eventually get swapped around with everyone.

Q. How do I build deeper friendships with my supper-swapping group?

A. Women have such a longing for friendship and such an amazing capacity to love. You'll be amazed how your friendships naturally deepen on their own as you swap suppers together. Supper swapping gives you a built-in framework for friendship. But you can help make it happen by scheduling a girls' night out once a month, a date night with your husbands a few times a year, and family get-togethers like picnics or parties when all the families come together.

Q. How can supper swapping open the door for relational evangelism?

A. If you form your supper-swapping group with other Christian women, you'll discover that your faith is deepened as you pray for one another and turn to each another in times of need. If you have women in your group who aren't Christians, be careful not to make them feel uncomfortable with your faith. Just be their friend and let your faith impact them positively.

Q. How can I witness to people outside my supper-swapping group?

A. One way is to have your group pray for other families when you get together, bringing those in need around you to the group's prayer chain. Also, on your cooking day, it's easy to make an extra meal to deliver to a family in need, reaching far beyond your front porch with your faith.

Q. What do I do if I have to cancel my meal one week because I have a sick child or an unforeseen circumstance?

A. When you first form your group, you can decide how best to handle these situations. Have a plan set up in advance, one you're all comfortable with.

When someone in our group has a life circumstance that prevents her from cooking, we give her the week off. We still deliver our meals to that family; she just doesn't deliver to us. It's actually a huge gift you can give each other when life gets crazy, as it does when you have kids. But some groups have decided that when that happens, they'll have pizza delivered to the families in the group to cover the meal. However, that could get quite expensive.

Q. How can I be honest about others' cooking without hurting their feelings?

A. There's a difference between loving honesty and hurtful truths. You must all agree at the outset that you'll be honest about what meals work, while remaining kind and respectful of others' feelings. Try to sandwich negative comments between compliments. "Sue, I liked the blueberry muffins you made last week. Were those from scratch? My kids weren't crazy about the vegetable soup, but they did love your meatloaf. Could you make that next month?"

Q. How do we handle summer vacation and Christmas break?

A. Since everyone in my group has school-age children, we follow the school calendar and swap meals during the school year, taking off Christmas break, spring break, and summer vacation. But some supper-swapping groups swap meals all year. Again, it's up to you.

Q. Where can I find recipes that work well for supper swapping?

A. Go to www.supperswapmom.com for all of your supper-swapping needs. You'll find tons of great recipes, printable meal calendars, advice from swapping moms across the country, and all the resources and links you'll need to make your supper-swapping group a huge success. Also, see the next chapter of this book for recipes that can help you get started.

Q. What if I still have questions you haven't answered in *The Great American Supper Swap*?

A. Please ask me. I'd love to help in any way I can. Visit supperswapmom.com to contact me. From one supper-swap mom to another—happy swapping!

Seventeen

RAVING RECIPES

Proven Supper-Swapping Recipes to

Get You Started

Supper swapping is about simplifying supper, not impressing your family and friends with gourmet meals. Tailor your recipes and meal calendars to meet your needs, tastes, and cooking styles.

The best way to start swapping is to begin with your own family-favorite recipes. As you settle into a supper-swapping routine, you'll discover what meals work best for the families in your group. Once you're feeling confident, you can begin blending in new recipes from cookbooks, magazines, and Web sites.

Here are several proven swapping recipes to get you started. For more *free* recipes that work great with supper swapping, or to exchange recipes with supper-swapping moms coast to coast, be sure to visit www.trishberg.com, and click on the supper-swapping link.

> In the house of the
> wise are stores of
> choice food and oil.
> PROVERBS 21:20

Baked Potato Haystacks (Teri Weaver)

Teri's family loves making Haystacks when extended family pops in for a visit. This meal is very popular in the Amish community because it's simple and allows for more social time and less time in the kitchen. So consider making this when your supper-swapping group meets for an evening of get-to-know-you family fun.

Ingredients:

10 potatoes, baked
1 head lettuce, shredded
1 lg. onion, chopped fine
1 – 16 oz. bag of baby carrots, finely chopped
1 – 18 oz. can sloppy joe sauce
2 lbs. lean ground beef, browned and drained
1 – 28 oz. can pork and beans
1 – 13 oz. bag Nacho Cheese Doritos, crushed
2 – 10 3/4 oz. cans cream of mushroom soup
2 T. milk
1 lb. Velveeta cheese

Directions:

1. Bake potatoes at 350 degrees for about an hour until tender.

2. Shred lettuce; chop onions and carrots fine. Put each in a separate serving bowl with a spoon. Set aside.

3. Place crushed Doritos in a separate serving bowl with a spoon. Set aside.

4. In a saucepan, combine sloppy joe sauce, ground beef, and pork and beans; heat until bubbly. Keep warm.

5. In a separate saucepan, dilute cream of mushroom soup with milk and Velveeta cheese on low heat until well blended. Keep warm.

6. At serving time, have guests begin with their baked potato on a large plate, sliced open and mashed with a fork. As they walk down the buffet line, they top their potato with the toppings of their choice in this order: sloppy joe; lettuce; onions; carrots; cheese sauce; ending with Doritos.

7. Haystacks get as large as you want, and you can make a whole meal out of them!

Serves 10.

Baked Spaghetti (Trish Berg)

Baked spaghetti is a kid-friendly meal that you can make ahead since it freezes well. It's also a great recipe to share with a neighbor or a friend in need. Great side dishes include garlic bread and fresh tossed salad.

Ingredients:

1 – 1 lb. box spaghetti

8 oz. mozzarella cheese

1 1/2 lbs. ground beef, cooked and drained

1 – 25 oz. jar spaghetti sauce

1 c. grated Parmesan cheese

2 eggs, beaten

1/2 stick butter or margarine, melted

1 – 10 3/4 oz. can cream of chicken soup

Directions:

1. Cook and drain spaghetti according to package directions. Set aside.

2. In electric skillet or large stove-top skillet, combine sauce and ground beef. Heat through for about 10 minutes.

3. Spread half the sauce mixture in a greased 9x13-inch glass baking pan.

4. Top with half the spaghetti noodles, then half the mozzarella cheese.

5. Repeat layers one more time.

6. In separate mixing bowl, blend the Parmesan cheese, eggs, butter, and soup.

7. Evenly spread soup mixture over spaghetti in pan.

8. Bake at 350 degrees for 45 to 60 minutes until hot and bubbly.

Serves 8.

Beef Enchiladas (Carla Bidlack)

In our supper-swapping group, we discovered over the years that each of us has a different cooking style and unique tastes. Carla and Kelly both make more Mexican food than the rest of us do, and swapping suppers with them has allowed our families to expand our tastes.

Ingredients:

1 c. ketchup

1/2 c. brown sugar

2 T. vinegar

1 T. Worcestershire sauce

1 T. soy sauce

1 t. prepared mustard

1/2 c. water

1 1/2 lbs. ground beef, cooked and drained

8 oz. shredded cheddar cheese

1 – 20 oz. pkg. lg. flour tortillas

Directions:

1. Combine first seven ingredients in sauce pan and cook until just boiling; set aside.

2. Put 3 to 4 tablespoons of ground beef in each tortilla. Using half the cheddar cheese, add 2 to 3 tablespoons of cheese into each tortilla. Roll tortillas.

3. Place rolled tortillas into a greased 9x13-inch glass baking pan. Cover with sauce and sprinkle with remaining shredded cheese.

4. Bake at 350 degrees for 20 to 30 minutes, until hot and bubbly.

Serves 6 to 8.

Beef Tips with Noodles (Nann Warren)

This is a great comfort-food meal that can be tailored to fit your own tastes. My family doesn't like mushrooms, but you could add them if you want to.

Ingredients:

2 lbs. beef stew meat

6 c. water, divided

1 stick butter

garlic, pepper, salt, soy sauce to taste

4 beef bouillon cubes

1 – 1 oz. pkg. dry onion soup mix

4 – 1 1/4 oz. pkts. brown gravy mix

1 – 16 oz. pkg. egg noodles

Directions:

1. Brown stew meat in an electric skillet or large stove-top skillet.

2. Add 2 cups of water and butter.

3. Add seasonings, beef bouillon, and onion soup mix.

4. Let meat simmer for 10 minutes in the electric skillet on 300 degrees or on medium heat on your stove top.

5. Add 2 cups of water to the meat; cook for 2 hours.

6. When meat is tender, add gravy packets and noodles along with remaining water.

7. When noodles are tender, meal is done.

Serves 6.

Breakfast Casserole (Kelly Manley)

We love this breakfast-for-dinner meal and always save leftovers for breakfast the next morning. Teri and I both make this casserole for Christmas morning brunch. It goes great with blueberry muffins.

Ingredients:

6 slices white bread, cubed

1 lb. bulk breakfast sausage, cooked and drained

8 eggs, slightly beaten

2 c. milk

1 t. salt

dash of pepper

1 t. dry mustard

1 c. sharp cheddar cheese, shredded

Directions:

1. Put cubed bread in a greased a 9x13-inch pan.

2. Mix in cooked sausage.

3. In separate bowl, combine eggs, milk, salt, pepper, and mustard until blended. Pour egg mixture over sausage and bread; toss lightly.

4. Sprinkle cheese on top.

5. Cover pan with foil and refrigerate for 12 hours or overnight.

6. Bake uncovered 35 minutes at 350 degrees.

Serves 6.

Cheesy Chicken Pot Pie (Trish Berg)

Cheesy Chicken Pot Pie will soon become one of your family favorites. It's simple to prepare and delicious to boot! If you have time, you can always make your pie crusts from scratch; however, if time is tight, frozen crusts work just as well.

Ingredients:

1 – 10 3/4 oz. can cream of chicken soup

1/2 c. onion, chopped fine

12 oz. sour cream

1/2 t. salt

4 oz. cheddar cheese, shredded

2 frozen pie crusts (one for bottom and one for top of pie)*

1/2 c. milk

4 oz. cream cheese, softened

1/4 c. Parmesan cheese, grated

1 egg

3 c. cooked chicken breast, cubed

1/2 - 1 lb. bag frozen mixed vegetables

1/2 - 1 lb. bag frozen hash browns

Directions:
1. In large mixing bowl, blend together everything except chicken and vegetables.
2. Fold in chicken and vegetables.
3. Pour filling into one pie crust. Cover with a second crust, sealing edges.
4. With a sharp knife cut several small slits in the top of the pie crust for ventilation.
5. Bake uncovered at 375 degrees for about an hour, until top of pie crust is slightly brown.
6. If your families are larger, you can either make each family 2 pies, or double the recipe and place it a 9x13-inch baking dish.

Single recipe serves 4; double recipe serves 8.

*If you prefer homemade pie crusts, here is a quick recipe for a two-crust pie:

Ingredients:
2/3 c. plus 2 T. shortening

2 c. all-purpose flour

1 t. salt

4 to 5 T. cold water, added as needed

Directions:

1. In mixing bowl, cut shortening into flour and salt until particles are the size of coarse crumbs.
2. Sprinkle with cold water 1 tablespoon at a time, tossing with fork until flour is moist and crust cleans sides of bowl. (Add more water if needed, sparingly.)
3. Gather crust into a ball, divide into 2 parts.
4. On lightly floured counter, roll each half into circle 2 inches larger than upside-down pie pan.
5. Use one crust for the bottom of the pie and one crust for the top of the pie, cutting small slits in the top for ventilation.

Chicken Penne Pasta (Teri Weaver)

Teri found this recipe on a fluke. It's just a different twist on a basic macaroni and cheese recipe with added meat to make it a more well-rounded meal. We love it when Teri makes her Grape Delight (see page 227) to go with Chicken Penne Pasta.

Ingredients:

16 oz. penne pasta, uncooked

16 oz. Velveeta cheese, cubed

18 oz. sour cream

1/2 c. milk

2 1/2 c. boneless, skinless chicken, cubed

Directions:

1. Cook pasta as directed on package, drain, and set aside.
2. In saucepan, cook cheese, sour cream, and milk over low to medium heat, stirring constantly, for 5 minutes or until cheese melts.
3. Fold in cooked pasta and chicken; cook and stir until heated.

4. Place in 9x13-inch greased baking dish. Bake uncovered at 350
   degrees for 20 minutes until heated through and top is lightly
   browned.

Serves 6.

Chicken Quesadillas (Trish Berg)

The husbands in our group love this quick and easy Mexican recipe. You can use mild or hot salsa and add rice or refried beans on the side.

Ingredients:
   4 to 6 boneless, skinless chicken breasts, cooked and cubed
   1 – 16 oz. jar salsa (mild, medium, or hot)
   8 oz. sour cream
   1 – 10 count pkg. flour tortillas
   8 oz. shredded cheddar cheese
   1/4 c. oil

Directions:
   1. Place cubed chicken in electric skillet or large stove-top skillet.
   2. Add salsa, and heat through, stirring.
   3. Remove chicken mixture and place in bowl.
   4. Unplug and clean skillet before continuing.
   5. Reheat skillet with thin layer of oil for frying.
   6. Take one tortilla and spoon three tablespoons of chicken mixture on top, and add sprinkling of shredded cheddar cheese.
   7. Fold tortilla over to form a seam.
   8. Place seam-side down in hot oil.
   9. Place 4 to 6 tortillas in skillet at a time depending on how many will fit.

10. Turn tortillas over once when side is slightly brown.
11. Remove from skillet and place in sprayed baking dish in single layer.
12. When ready to serve, reheat in oven on 175 degrees until warm.
13. Serve with sour cream on top.

Serves 6.

Chicken Roll-ups (Kelly Manley)

Everyone in our group requests Kelly's Chicken Roll-ups when we plan our meal calendars. It's a kid-friendly meal that moms and dads will love as well. It goes great with corn on the cob and fresh veggies and dip. Serve Kool-Aid Fruit (see page 229) for dessert.

Ingredients:

4 boneless, skinless chicken breasts, cubed
16 oz. Velveeta cheese
2 tubes refrigerator crescent rolls
1 – 10 oz. can cream of chicken soup
1 c. milk
1/4 t. paprika (optional)

Directions:

1. Cook chicken breasts and cut into 16 strips.
2. Cut cheese into 16 strips.
3. Roll up 1 strip of chicken and 1 strip of cheese in each crescent roll.
4. Place rolls in greased 9x13-inch baking dish.
5. In separate bowl, mix soup and milk together; pour over rolls.
6. Sprinkle with paprika if desired.
7. Bake uncovered at 350 degrees for 50 minutes.

Serves 6.

Creamy Lasagna (Sylvia Koch)

This is a unique twist on lasagna. Nann's mom, Sylvia, makes this creamy dish to all of our rave reviews. It's so moist, it will melt in your mouth. Great sides include tossed salad and garlic bread.

Ingredients:

2 lbs. lean ground beef

garlic, pepper, salt, dried green peppers, and onion powder
    seasoning to taste

8 oz. cream cheese

1 lb. lasagna noodles

1 – 16 oz. jar spaghetti sauce

16 oz. mozzarella cheese

Directions:

1. Brown ground beef and drain; add seasonings and sauté, stirring constantly, for 2 minutes.
2. Place brick of cream cheese into ground beef and let simmer until cream cheese is fully melted.
3. Cook noodles according to package directions; drain.
4. Layer in greased 9x13-inch pan: one-half of noodles, pasta sauce, and beef mixture.
5. Repeat layers. Top with mozzarella cheese. Bake at 350 degrees for 1 hour.

Serves 6.

Golfer's Stew (Carla Bidlack)

This is a fantastic recipe to deliver in the morning to your supper-swapping girlfriends for them to simmer throughout the day. The aroma will fill their kitchens with warmth. It goes great with the Quick and Easy Yeast Rolls (see page 224).

Ingredients:

3 lbs. stew beef

5 carrots, diced

5 potatoes, diced

1 lg. onion, diced

1 - 14 1/2 oz. can peas

1 - 10 3/4 oz. can cream of mushroom soup

1 - 10 3/4 oz. can tomato soup

Directions:

1. Layer ingredients in order listed in a Dutch oven.
2. Bake covered at 275 degrees for 5 hours.

Serves 8.

Grilled Chicken Oriental Salad
(Trish Berg)

When I worked as a marketing manager, next door to my office was this great deli. Several days a week I would order its chicken oriental salad. It came in a huge bowl and was served with a lemon crumb muffin the size of a Volkswagen. So, one day I decided to write down all the ingredients and make it myself at home. It's become a popular family meal.

Ingredients:

1 head lettuce, washed and shredded

6 boneless, skinless chicken breasts, cooked and cubed

6 oz. slivered almonds

1 – 8 oz. can mandarin oranges, drained

1 to 2 green onions, washed and chopped

1 – 12 oz. bag chow mein noodles

1 – 16 oz. jar sweet and sour poppy-seed salad dressing

Directions:

1. Place shredded lettuce in large salad bowl.
2. Top with cubed chicken, almonds, oranges, green onion, and noodles.
3. Serve with poppy-seed salad dressing.
4. If delivering early in the day for your supper-swapping meal, keep all ingredients in separate zippered plastic bags for each family to assemble at suppertime.
5. If you are in a pinch for time, you can substitute cut-up breaded chicken patties for the cubed chicken.

Serves 6.

Ham Loaf (Mary Ann Berg)

Until I met Mike, I had never had Ham Loaf or even knew it existed. My mother-in-law, Mary Ann, makes this dish for many of our family gatherings and serves it with Cheesy Potatoes (see page 211) and fresh corn on the side.

Ingredients:

2 lbs. ground ham loaf mix (or 1 lb. ground ham and 1 lb. ground pork)

2 eggs

1 c. fine bread crumbs

1 c. milk

1/2 t. salt

1/2 t. pepper

Glaze:

1/2 c. brown sugar

1/4 c. vinegar

1/2 c. water

1 t. mustard

Directions:

1. In a large mixing bowl, hand mix the ground ham, eggs, bread crumbs, milk, salt, and pepper until well blended.
2. Form into a loaf, and place in a greased 9x13-inch glass pan.
3. In a pot, combine all the glaze ingredients and bring to a boil; cook for 5 minutes. Pour over ham loaf.
4. Bake at 350 degrees for 45 minutes.

Serves 6.

Homemade Pizza (Trish Berg)

We started a wonderful family tradition years ago of eating homemade pizza and watching a DVD every Sunday night. The kids always look forward to our family time and are more willing to get ready for their school week when they know that pizza and a movie are coming before bedtime. This recipe is one of my favorites.

Ingredients:

Crust:

2 1/2 t. yeast (or 1 pkg. quick-rise yeast)

1/2 t. sugar

1 t. salt

2 c. warm water

5 c. flour

Toppings:

1 – 14 oz. can pizza sauce

12 oz. shredded mozzarella cheese

8 oz. shredded cheddar cheese

Pizza toppings of your choice:

Pepperoni, cooked sausage, green peppers, mushrooms, black olives, ham, or even pineapple chunks.

Directions:

1. Mix yeast, salt, sugar, and warm water in large mixing bowl. (I use my Kitchen Aid.)
2. Whisk together, and set aside for 10 minutes to rise.
3. Add flour gradually as you blend. Dough will become stiff and you may need to hand knead it after awhile (or use the dough hook on your Kitchen Aid stand mixer).
4. Cover bowl, and set aside in warm place to rise for about 1 hour.
5. Butter your hands. Divide dough into 2 balls, and push flat onto large greased round pizza pan.
6. Top with pizza sauce, cheese, and your favorite pizza toppings.
7. You can cover the pizza and freeze it for later use, or deliver it for your swapping meal uncooked so each family can pull it out of the oven freshly baked.
8. Bake pizzas at 450 degrees for 10 to 20 minutes.

Serves 6.

When Carla left our group several years back, we kept this recipe going because we loved it so much. Serve it with Party Potatoes (see page 212) on the side so you can soak up some of the extra sauce as you eat your mashed potatoes.

Ingredients:

1 lb. meatballs (You can buy premade meatballs at most groceries stores and Wal-Marts.)

1 lb. kielbasa, precooked and sliced

Sauce:

1 – 10 3/4 oz. can tomato soup

1 1/4 c. brown sugar

1/4 c. vinegar

1/8 t. cinnamon

Directions:

1. Lay meatballs and kielbasa in a single layer on a greased 9x13-inch glass baking dish.
2. In separate mixing bowl, blend all sauce ingredients; pour over meat.
3. Bake at 350 degrees for 30 to 40 minutes until hot and bubbly.
4. Or you could place meat and sauce in Crock-Pot on low setting for about 12 hours.

Serves 6.

When Kelly made Pan Burritos for our group last month, I froze the leftovers. Just this week I reheated them in my microwave, topped them with a dollop of sour cream, and had the best homemade lunch ever. Who says you need a name-brand frozen meal?

Ingredients:

1 – 10 oz. jar enchilada sauce

3 c. water

12 oz. tomato paste

1 garlic clove, minced

1/4 t. pepper

salt to taste

2 lbs. ground beef

9 – 9-inch flour tortillas

16 oz. shredded taco cheese

16 oz. refried beans, warmed

Toppings:

sour cream (optional)

taco sauce (optional)

Directions:

1. In a saucepan, combine enchilada sauce, water, tomato paste, garlic, pepper, and salt.
2. Simmer for 15 to 20 minutes.
3. In a skillet, brown and drain the beef.
4. Stir 1/3 of the sauce in with the beef. Spread another 1/3 on the bottom of a greased 9x13-inch baking pan.
5. Place three tortillas over sauce in pan, tearing to fit bottom of pan.

6. Spoon half of meat mixture over tortillas; sprinkle with 1 1/2 cups cheese.
7. Add three more tortillas.
8. Spread refried beans over tortillas.
9. Top with remaining meat.
10. Sprinkle with 1 1/2 cups cheese.
11. Layer remaining tortillas on top.
12. Top with the remaining 1/3 of enchilada sauce. Sprinkle with remaining cheese.
13. Bake uncovered at 350 degrees for 35 to 45 minutes. Let stand 10 minutes before cutting.
14. Serve with taco sauce and sour cream if desired.

Serves 6.

Pasta Ham Bake (Amy Frantz)

If you like pasta salad, you'll love this warmer version. Pasta Ham Bake is a wonderful twist on an old favorite with a delicious texture. It goes great with breadsticks.

Ingredients:
1 lb. tube pasta
5 cloves garlic, minced
1/4 t. basil
1/2 c. Parmesan cheese
16 oz. mayonnaise
16 oz. shredded mozzarella cheese
2 c. ham, cooked and cubed
1 – 14 1/2 oz. can chopped tomatoes, drained

Directions:

1. Cook pasta according to package directions; drain and set aside.
2. In large mixing bowl, blend garlic, basil, Parmesan cheese, mayonnaise, and 1/2 of the mozzarella cheese.
3. Place pasta, ham, and tomatoes in greased 9x13-inch baking dish.
4. Pour Parmesan sauce on top and lightly fold in.
5. Top with remaining mozzarella cheese.
6. Bake covered at 350 degrees for 20 minutes, uncover, and bake an additional 5 to 10 minutes.

Serves 6.

Poppy-Seed Chicken (Carla Bidlack)

Even though my supper-swapping group currently has only three families, I usually make four pans of Poppy-Seed Chicken since it freezes so well. Then I can bake it on a busy nonswapping night or share it with a family in need without any added fuss or muss. Serve with Party Potatoes (see page 212).

Ingredients:

6 boneless, skinless chicken breasts, cooked and cubed
1 – 10 3/4 oz. can cream of mushroom soup
8 oz. cream cheese

Topping:

1 sleeve Ritz or Hi-Ho crackers, crushed
6 T. butter or margarine, melted
1 T. poppy seeds

Directions:

1. Place cubed chicken in greased 9x13-inch baking dish.
2. In separate bowl, mix soup and sour cream; spread over chicken.
3. Mix topping in separate bowl and sprinkle over chicken mixture.
4. Bake at 350 degrees for 20 to 30 minutes, until bubbly and heated through.

Serves 6.

Saucy Meatballs (Kathy Thut)

These meatballs are great for any party or gathering. You can make large meatballs for a meal or serve small ones with toothpicks. They go great with baked potatoes.

Ingredients:

2 lbs. ground beef
2 eggs
2 t. salt
1/4 t. pepper
1 c. bread crumbs

Sauce:

14 oz. container ketchup
10 oz. jar grape jelly
1/2 c. onion, minced

Directions:

1. Mix meatball ingredients together and form into balls about 1 inch in diameter; place meatballs into greased 9x13-inch baking dish; set aside.
2. In large saucepan, mix ketchup, grape jelly, and onion; cook over

medium heat, stirring, until jelly is melted.

3. Pour over meatballs.

4. Bake uncovered at 350 degrees for 45 to 60 minutes or in slow cooker on low for 4 hours.

Serves 6.

Shepherd's Pie (Nann Warren)

Another kid favorite in our house, this meal is a great comfort food that warms you inside and out. A great side is fresh fruit or Grape Delight (see page 227).

Ingredients:

2 lbs. ground beef

garlic, pepper, salt, and onion powder seasoning to taste

4 - 1 oz. pkt. brown beef gravy mix

2 - 10 3/4 oz. cans green beans

3 lbs. white potatoes, peeled and cut in half

1 - 1 oz. pkg. dry onion soup mix

16 oz. shredded cheddar cheese

Directions:

1. Brown and drain ground beef; add dry onion soup mix and other seasonings and let simmer on low for 10 minutes.

2. Add gravy mix to the beef, following packet directions for how much water to add; simmer until gravy begins to thicken.

3. Add green beans to the hamburger mixture and simmer.

4. Place hamburger mixture in the bottom of a greased 9x13-inch baking dish; set aside.

5. Boil potatoes until tender; drain. Mash potatoes adding milk and butter until creamy like typical mashed potatoes.

6. Spread the mashed potatoes evenly on top of the hamburger mixture, covering it all.
7. Top with the cheddar cheese.
8. Bake at 350 degrees for 1 hour.

Serves 6.

Sunday French Toast (Kelly Manley)

We serve sausage with this delightful breakfast-for-dinner meal. And the leftovers, of course, are good for breakfast in the morning.

Ingredients:
8 slices of bread, thick
2/3 c. brown sugar
1/2 c. melted butter
2 t. cinnamon
6 eggs
2 c. milk

Directions:
1. Combine sugar and cinnamon, and sprinkle on bottom of a coated 9x13-inch glass baking dish.
2. Melt butter and drizzle over sugar mixture.
3. In separate mixing bowl, beat eggs and milk until blended.
4. Dip bread in egg mixture, letting extra egg mixture drip back into mixing bowl, then lay bread slices in single layer over top of sugar mixture.
5. After all 8 slices of bread are dipped and laid out, if there is egg mixture left, evenly pour it over the bread before baking.

6. Bake at 350 degrees for 25 to 30 minutes, until heated through, warm and bubbly.

Serves 6 to 8.

Yumazetti (Teri Weaver)

Teri's son, Tad, loves Yumazetti. She makes it for him every year on his birthday for a special treat. You probably have most of the ingredients on hand in your pantry, so it makes for an easy supper on a nonswapping night.

Ingredients:
2 lbs. ground beef

1 – 8 oz. pkg. pasta noodles

1 – 10 3/4 oz. can cream of mushroom soup

1 – 10 3/4 oz. can cream of celery soup

1 – 16 oz. jar pizza sauce

1 lb. Velveeta cheese, sliced

Directions:
1. Brown hamburger; drain and set aside.
2. Cook pasta according to package directions; drain and set aside.
3. Put beef and noodles into a greased 9x13-inch baking dish; toss together.
4. In separate mixing bowl, combine soups and pizza sauce. Pour over beef and noodle mixture.
5. Place cheese slices on top.
6. Bake at 350 degrees for 45 minutes.

Serves 6.

Amish Noodles (Teri Weaver)

My husband, Mike, loves Teri's Amish Noodles so much that he requests that she bring them as a side dish with every supper she delivers.

Ingredients:
  1/4 c. butter
  2 – 14 1/2 oz. cans chicken broth
  1 T. chicken soup base
  1 – 8 oz. bag medium flat noodles

Directions:
  1. Using a heavy-bottom pot, brown butter.
  2. Add chicken broth and chicken soup base; bring to a boil.
  3. Add noodles; return to a boil.
  4. Immediately cover and turn off burner.
  5. Let stand for approximately 30 minutes.
  6. Stir well before serving.

Serves 6.

Baked Corn (Carla Bidlack)

Kelly loves to serve this recipe as a side dish with her famous Pan Burritos (see page 203). It's extremely easy to assemble, and we all look forward to the sweet corn complimenting the Mexican fare.

Ingredients:

- 1 – 14 1/2 oz. can cream-style corn
- 1 – 14 1/2 oz. can whole-kernel corn
- 1/3 c. sugar
- 2 eggs, beaten
- 1 – 8 oz. container sour cream
- 1/4 c. butter or margarine
- 1 – 7 oz. box corn-muffin mix

Directions:

1. Mix together the two corns and sugar.
2. Beat eggs in a separate bowl, then add sour cream.
3. Add egg and sour-cream mixture to corn.
4. Cut butter into small slices, add to corn.
5. Stir in half of the corn-muffin mix.
6. Pour into a greased 9x13-inch dish.
7. Sprinkle the remaining muffin mix on top.
8. Bake 30 to 40 minutes at 350 degrees.

Serves 8.

Cheesy Potatoes (Mary Ann Berg)

This side dish is one of my family's favorites. It freezes so well that it also works as a great make-ahead dish for church potlucks. My mother-in-law always makes Cheesy Potatoes to go along with her homemade Ham Loaf (see page 199).

Ingredients:

- 1 – 2 lbs. bag frozen hash browns
- 1 – 10 3/4 oz. can cream of chicken soup

1 – 8 oz. container sour cream

8 oz. shredded cheddar cheese

Directions:

1. Thaw hash browns.
2. In a large bowl, mix all the ingredients together, tossing with a wooden spoon.
3. Spread in a greased 9x13-inch baking dish.
4. Bake uncovered at 350 degrees for about an hour, until heated through and cheese is melted.

Serves 6.

Party Potatoes (Carla Bidlack)

Nothing is quite as comforting as a heaping helping of home-made mashed potatoes. Since mashed potatoes usually dry out fast, we had to find a recipe that would work well with our make-ahead suppers. These potatoes stay creamy and smooth and satisfy even the toughest critic. Very good served with Saucy Meatballs (see page 206).

Ingredients:

3 to 5 lbs. potatoes

1/2 c. butter or margarine

16 oz. sour cream

8 oz. cream cheese

salt and pepper to taste

8 to 10 oz. shredded cheddar cheese

Directions:

1. Peel potatoes and cut in half. Boil in large pot until tender; drain.
2. Add butter, sour cream, cream cheese, salt, and pepper; whip until smooth and creamy.
3. Spoon into coated 9x13-inch glass baking dish. Sprinkle with cheddar cheese.
4. Bake at 350 degrees for 20 to 25 minutes or until heated through.
5. Can be frozen before baking for later use.

Serves 6 to 8.

Salads

Broccoli and Cauliflower Salad (Teri Weaver)

If you're going to the farmer's market, pick up all your ingredients for this tasty salad. It's a wonderful way to get your kids to eat more vegetables.

Ingredients:

1 bunch broccoli
1 head cauliflower
1 c. carrots, shredded
1 pt. mayonnaise
1/3 c. sugar
1 c. shredded cheddar cheese
1/2 c. bacon bits

Directions:

1. Wash and chop broccoli and cauliflower into very small pieces. Place in large bowl and add shredded carrots.
2. In separate mixing bowl, blend mayonnaise, sugar, cheese, and bacon bits. Pour over broccoli, cauliflower, and carrots. Fold until well coated.
3. Chill until ready to serve.

Serves 6.

Mandarin Salad (Carla Bidlack)

I made this salad when we had Mike's baseball coaches over for a picnic—and they practically licked the bowl clean! It has a sweet and crunchy taste that everyone will like.

Ingredients:

1/2 t. salt
dash of pepper
2 t. sugar
dash of Tabasco sauce
1/4 c. canola oil
1 T. parsley, chopped
2 T. vinegar
1 – 10 oz. bag Italian salad blend
2 whole green onions, chopped
1/2 c. celery, chopped
1/2 c. slivered almonds
1 – 11 oz. can mandarin oranges, drained
1 crisp apple, chopped
1/2 c. Craisins (dried cranberries in a bag)
1 c. crunchy Chinese rice or Chow Mein noodles (optional)

Directions:

1. Mix together the first seven ingredients; chill.
2. Toss lettuce, onions, and celery together in large salad bowl.
3. Just before serving, add almonds and fruit; toss with dressing.

Serves 6.

Oriental Slaw (Carla Bidlack)

Who would have ever thought you could find a tasty way to use ramen noodles!

Ingredients:

1 – 10 oz. bag grated cabbage
1/2 c. sesame seeds
1/2 c. slivered almonds
2 – 3 oz. pkg. ramen chicken noodles (save one seasoning pkt.)

Dressing:

1/2 c. oil
3/4 c. sugar
1/4 c. vinegar
2 T. soy sauce
1 seasoning pkt. from the noodles

Directions:

1. In 9x13-inch baking dish, combine cabbage, sesame seeds, and almonds; toast in oven at 350 degrees for 7 minutes. Pour into large bowl.
2. By hand, break up noodles and toss into cabbage mixture. Store in the pan or in a large zippered plastic bag.
3. In mixing bowl, blend oil, sugar, vinegar, soy sauce, and

seasoning packet. Store in a plastic container.

4. About 30 minutes before supper, toss cabbage mixture with sauce and serve immediately.

Serves 6.

Twenty-Four-Hour Salad
(Mary Ann Berg)

This salad can be made a day ahead, and you don't have to carry dressing since the dressing is already on the salad.

Ingredients:

1 head lettuce, torn
1/2 c. celery, diced
1/2 c. green peppers, diced
1/2 c. onion, diced
1/2 bag frozen peas
2 c. mayonnaise
2 T. sugar
8 oz. shredded cheddar cheese
6 to 8 bacon strips, cooked and crumbled

Directions:

1. Layer in order listed, lettuce, celery, peppers, onion, and peas in a large 9x13-inch glass baking dish.
2. Spread mayonnaise on top evenly.
3. Sprinkle sugar over top of mayonnaise and top with bacon and shredded cheese.
4. Cover and refrigerate overnight. Serve cold.

Serves 8.

Autumn Soup (Teri Weaver)

Before Teri's family heads to the high school football game to watch Tad march in the band at halftime, they enjoy warm Autumn Soup with corn bread on the side, apple cider to drink, and pumpkin pie for dessert.

Ingredients:

8 to 10 slices bacon, cooked and crumbled

1 t. butter or margarine

10 medium red potatoes, diced

12 baby carrots, diced

1 c. chopped onion

2 1/2 c. water

2 T. chicken bouillon

5 c. milk

2 c. frozen corn

1 1/2 t. pepper

1/4 c. flour

12 oz. shredded cheddar cheese

Directions:

1. In large saucepan, melt butter. Add onions, potatoes, and carrots; sauté until tender.

2. Add water and bouillon. Bring to a boil. Reduce heat and simmer 15 to 20 minutes.

3. Stir in milk, corn, and pepper; cook 5 minutes.

4. In a small bowl, combine flour with enough water to make a

paste; whisk until smooth, then add to soup.

5. Remove from heat and stir in cheese until melted.

6. At mealtime, sprinkle each bowl of soup with bacon crumbs.

Serves 6.

Broccoli Cheese Soup (Mary Ann Berg)

Our kids request Broccoli Cheese Soup as much as they do pizza. It is simple to make and is a wonderful way to get your kids to eat their vegetables!

Ingredients:

6 c. boiling water

1 to 2 t. chicken bouillon

1 – 8 oz. bag medium egg noodles

2 lbs. Velveeta cheese

6 c. milk

20 oz. frozen, chopped broccoli, thawed

Directions:

1. Bring water to a boil. Add chicken bouillon and noodles, and cook until tender.

2. In a separate sauce pan, heat milk and sliced Velveeta until blended and heated through; pour into soup base.

3. Add broccoli, and simmer for 20 to 30 minutes until broccoli is tender.

Serves 8.

Cheeseburger Soup (Trish Berg)

My sister gave me this recipe several years ago. My kids love its cheesy taste, and I get to sneak in some vegetables without hearing "yuck." We love eating it with fresh baked rolls and fresh fruit.

Ingredients:
- 3/4 c. chopped onion
- 3/4 c. shredded carrots
- 1 t. dried basil
- 1 t. dried parsley
- 4 T. butter or margarine, divided
- 3 c. chicken broth
- 4 c. potatoes, peeled and diced
- 1/2 lb. ground beef, browned and drained
- 1/4 c. all-purpose flour
- 8 oz. cubed Velveeta cheese
- 1 1/2 c. milk
- 1/2 t. salt
- 1/2 t. pepper
- 1/4 c. sour cream

Directions:
1. In large saucepan or stockpot, sauté onions, carrots, basil, and parsley in 1 tablespoon butter until tender, about 10 minutes.
2. Add chicken broth, potatoes, and beef, and bring to a boil.
3. Reduce heat; cover and simmer for 10 to 12 minutes or until potatoes are tender.
4. In a small skillet, melt remaining butter. Add flour; stir for 3 to 5 minutes or until bubbly. Add to soup.
5. Bring soup to a boil again and cook for 2 minutes.

6. Reduce heat to low and add cheese, milk, salt, and pepper. Cook and stir until cheese melts.

7. Remove from heat and blend in sour cream.

Serves 6.

Easy Baked Potato Soup (Trish Berg)

This recipe is a great way to make use of leftover baked potatoes. It's simple to prepare and goes well with Lemon Crumb Muffins (see page 223).

Ingredients:

3 to 4 medium potatoes, baked, peeled, and diced

5 bacon strips, cooked and crumbled

2 – 10 3/4 oz. cans cream of potato soup, undiluted

3 1/2 c. milk

2 t. garlic powder

2 t. Worcestershire sauce

1/2 t. onion powder

1 c. sour cream

1 c. shredded cheddar cheese

Directions:

1. In large stockpot, add all ingredients except sour cream and cheddar cheese. Cook uncovered for ten minutes on medium heat until heated through.

2. Stir in sour cream; cook for 1 to 2 minutes until heated. Do not boil.

3. Garnish with shredded cheddar cheese and crumbled bacon.

Serves 8.

This was one of Carla's supper-swapping recipes that we all loved and looked forward to. So when she left our group, we asked if we could keep the recipe! There's nothing better than the smell of warm soup simmering to get your family to the dinner table. Serve with warm bread.

Ingredients:

1/2 lb. ground beef

1/2 c. onion, chopped

1 1/2 qt. tomato juice

1 –14 oz. can diced tomatoes

1 pkg. taco seasoning

2 to 3 c. water

salt and pepper to taste

1 – 10 1/2 oz. can pork and beans

1 – 10 3/4 oz. can kernel corn, drained

Toppings (optional):

Shredded cheddar cheese

Sour cream

Tortilla chips

Directions:

1. In an electric or large stove-top skillet, brown ground beef. Drain; return to pan.
2. Add onion. Over medium high, cook until tender.
3. Place beef and onions into soup stockpot.
4. Add remaining ingredients and simmer 15 to 20 minutes until heated through. It can also be put in slow cooker on low for 4 to 6 hours.

5. Serve with shredded cheddar cheese, chips, and sour cream to top with.

Serves 6.

Breads and Muffins

Double Quick Dinner Rolls (Trish Berg)

One of my friends from MOPS (Mothers of Preschoolers) passed this easy recipe on to me. This recipe is so simple, you'll be able to serve your family fresh-from-the-oven bread whenever you want!

Ingredients:
> 2 1/2 t. active dry yeast (or 1 pkt.)
> 1 c. warm water
> 2 T. sugar
> 1 t. salt
> 1 egg
> 2 T. butter, melted
> 2 1/4 c. flour

Directions:
1. Dissolve yeast in water.
2. Add sugar, salt, egg, butter, and half of flour; blend.
3. Add remaining flour; mix.
4. Allow dough to rise for one hour. (Dough will be moist and sticky like wallpaper paste.)
5. Spoon dough into greased muffin tins.

6. Let rise again for 30 to 60 minutes.

7. Bake at 400 degrees for 15 to 20 minutes or until brown on top.

8. Brush with butter; serve warm.

Yields 12 rolls.

Lemon Crumb Muffins (Trish Berg)

These muffins are a great with any soup or salad and satisfy everyone's sweet tooth. We love serving them as a side dish to Autumn Soup (see page 217), and we never seem to have any leftovers since the kids practically lick their plates.

Ingredients:

Muffin Batter:

2 1/2 c. self-rising flour

1/4 t. baking powder

1/2 c. sugar

2 T. grated lemon rind

3/4 c. buttermilk

1 1/2 t. vanilla extract

2 eggs, beaten

1/2 c. butter, melted

Streusel:

3/4 c. sugar

3/4 c. flour

1/4 c. butter, softened

In separate bowl, blend dry ingredients together, then cream in butter until smooth. Set aside.

Lemon Glaze:

  1/4 c. sugar

  3 T. lemon juice

  In separate bowl, stir together until sugar is dissolved. Set aside.

Directions:

1. Mix dry ingredients and lemon rind together. In separate bowl, whisk buttermilk, vanilla, and eggs together, then pour into dry ingredients. Using a metal spoon, stir until the mixture is just combined. Do not over mix; batter should be lumpy.
2. Spoon the mixture into coated muffin pan, filling each cup about 3/4 full.
3. Top with streusel and bake at 350 degrees for 10 to 12 minutes or until a toothpick comes out clean when inserted into the center of a muffin. Cool in the pan for 5 to 10 minutes. Carefully lift out and cool on wire rack.
4. Drizzle cooled muffins with lemon glaze.

Yields 12 muffins.

Quick and Easy Yeast Rolls (Trish Berg)

On a cold winter's night with the wind whistling outside your window, there is nothing that warms your home more than fresh-baked bread. I've always loved homemade bread, but never had the time to bake it. This recipe is as simple as it gets.

Ingredients:

  2 pkg. active dry yeast (or about 4 1/2 t.)

  1 1/2 c. warm water

  3 1/2 T. sugar

  4 T. oil

1 t. salt

2 eggs

5 to 5 1/2 c. flour

3 T. soft butter to brush on top

Directions:

1. In a large bowl, dissolve yeast in warm water.
2. Add remaining ingredients in the order listed, except flour; stir.
3. Add 2 cups of flour; blend.
4. Let the dough rise in a warm place for 15 minutes.
5. Stir the batter down and add the remaining flour.
6. Knead for about 3 minutes.
7. Divide the dough into 16 pieces, and shape into balls.
8. Put dough balls on greased cookie sheet and brush with melted butter.
9. Cover and let rise for 25 minutes.
10. Bake at 425 degrees for 12 to 15 minutes until golden brown.
11. Remove from oven and brush with additional butter.
12. Serve warm.

Serves 8.

Desserts

Cake Brownies (Teri Weaver)

These are positively the best brownies you will ever eat. They are doubly delicious and very, very moist! And we all know nothing makes your day go better than a smidgen of chocolate.

Ingredients:

1/2 c. butter, softened

1 c. sugar

4 eggs

1 – 16 oz. can chocolate syrup

1 t. vanilla

1 c. flour

1/2 t. salt

Glaze:

1 c. sugar

1/3 c. butter

1/3 c. milk

2/3 c. semisweet chocolate chips

2/3 c. miniature marshmallows

Directions:

1. In a mixing bowl, cream butter and sugar; add eggs, one at a time, beating well after each addition.
2. Beat in chocolate syrup and vanilla.
3. Add flour and salt until blended.
4. Pour into greased 11x17x1-inch jellyroll pan and bake at 350 degrees for 20 to 25 minutes; set aside to cool.
5. In small saucepan, combine sugar, butter, and milk. Bring to a boil and cook until the sugar is dissolved.
6. Remove from heat; stir in chocolate chips and marshmallows until melted.
7. Pour over brownies and spread evenly.

Yields 36 brownies.

Dresden Pumpkin Crunch (Amy Frantz)

This dessert will have kids and grown-ups alike asking for it all year long. We love to savor it with a warm cup of coffee or a tall glass of ice-cold milk.

Ingredients:

1 - 15 oz. can pumpkin

3 eggs

1 1/2 c. sugar

1- 14 oz. can sweetened condensed milk

4 t. pumpkin spice

1/2 t. salt

1 - 18 1/4 oz. box yellow cake mix, dry

1 c. pecans, crushed

1 c. butter, melted

Directions:

1. In a large mixing bowl, mix the first 6 ingredients.
2. Pour into a greased and floured 9x13-inch baking pan.
3. Sprinkle the dry cake mix over the mixture.
4. Top with crushed pecans.
5. Drizzle with melted butter.
6. Bake at 350 degrees for 40 to 50 minutes.

Serves 8.

Grape Delight (Teri Weaver)

After our family watched *The Lion, the Witch and the Wardrobe*, Colin began referring to Grape Delight as Turkish Delight!

Though I've never tasted Turkish Delight, Teri's Grape Delight is just as tempting, I'm sure!

Ingredients:

Crust:
1/3 c. butter, melted

1 c. powdered sugar

1 sleeve graham crackers (coarsely crushed)

Cream-Cheese Topping:
8 oz. cream cheese

1 c. powdered sugar

1 c. sour cream

8 oz. frozen whipped topping, thawed

Filling:
1 – 12 oz. can frozen 100% grape juice

3 juice cans water

3 c. sugar

1 c. clear gelatin powder

1 1/2 to 2 c. water

Directions:

1. In large mixing bowl, mix crushed graham crackers, melted butter, and 1 c. powdered sugar. Press in greased 9x13-inch pan; set aside.

2. In a separate large mixing bowl, blend together cream cheese, 1 c. powdered sugar, sour cream, and whipped topping. Pour over crust.

3. In large saucepan, combine 1 can frozen grape juice, 3 c. water, and sugar; bring to a boil.

4. Reduce heat. Add clear gelatin powder and 1 1/2 to 2 cups of water.

5. Bring to a boil again, then reduce heat and simmer for a few minutes.

6. Remove from heat and let cool. Pour over cream-cheese topping and refrigerate.

Serves 6.

Kool-Aid Fruit (Teri Weaver)

This old Amish favorite comes from Teri's husband, Jerry, who grew up in an Amish home. His family remains Amish and shares many delightful recipes with Teri that she passes on to us. This dessert not only tastes good but also looks beautiful served in clear plastic disposable cups for family gatherings.

Ingredients:

4 to 5 c. fresh fruit of your choice, diced

Glaze:

1 1/4 c. sugar

1 pkg. tropical punch Kool-Aid

1/2 c. clear gelatin powder

4 c. water, divided

Directions:

1. In mixing bowl, combine sugar, Kool-Aid, clear gelatin powder, and 1 cup of water to make pastelike mixture.

2. In sauce pan, bring remaining 3 cups of water to a boil. Add paste mixture and boil 2 minutes; let cool completely.

3. Place fresh fruit in large bowl.

4. Pour glaze over fruit; fold until covered.

5. Store in refrigerator; serve cold.

Serves 6.

Orange Gelatin Salad (Kelly Manley)

This dessert is very creamy and sweet and goes good with just about any main dish. Kelly loves serving it with her Chicken Roll-ups (see page 196).

Ingredients:

2 – 3 oz. boxes of orange gelatin

2 c. boiling water

6 oz. frozen orange juice (partially thawed)

1 – 11 oz. can mandarin oranges

1 – 10 oz. can crushed pineapple, drained

Topping:

1 pkg. boxed whipped topping mix

1 – 3 oz. box instant vanilla pudding mix

1 c. milk

Directions:

1. Dissolve gelatin in boiling water.

2. Add partially thawed orange juice, mandarin oranges, and pineapple.

3. Let gelatin mixture set in refrigerator for a few hours.

4. Prepare whipped topping as instructed on box; add dry pudding mix and 1 cup of milk. Beat together.

5. Spread topping onto set gelatin.

6. Refrigerate until ready to serve.

Serves 6.

Peanut Butter Cereal Bars
(Carla Bidlack)

Carla made these cereal bars for a treat when our families vacationed together at the lake. The kids all gobbled them up (I ate my fair share too!). It was a good thing Carla and I took a power walk around the island to work off some of those extra calories!

Ingredients:
- 1/2 c. sugar
- 1/2 c. white Karo syrup
- 3/4 c. peanut butter
- 1/2 t. vanilla
- 3 c. corn flakes
- 1/2 c. chocolate chips
- 1 c. butterscotch chips

Directions:
1. In a large saucepan, combine sugar and syrup.
2. Bring to just a rolling boil; pull it off the stove.
3. Add peanut butter, vanilla, and cereal; stir.
4. Spread the mixture in a greased 8x8-inch pan.
5. Melt chocolate chips in microwave until melted (20 seconds).
6. Spread over top of cereal mixture.
7. Let cool. Freezes well for later use.

Serves 6.

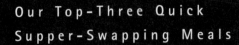
On those crazy, busy nights when you have soccer games, piano practice, and gymnastics to chauffer your kids to, here are our top-three quick-fix supper-swapping meals you can either make for your group or keep on hand for your own family on a nonswapping night.

#1 Pizza in a Pinch (Nann Warren)

Buy premade pizza dough, sauce, cheese, and the toppings of your choice. Follow the pizza-dough instructions, then assemble the pizzas and deliver. We all love the nights when Nann brings us her homemade pizzas!

#2 Taco Bar (Nann Warren)

Buy hard and soft taco shells, 2 lbs. ground beef, beef-taco seasoning, shredded cheese, sour cream, tomatoes, lettuce, and taco sauce. Brown your ground beef; drain and season with taco seasoning. Then put all your ingredients in plastic baggies and deliver a fresh taco bar. It makes for a winning family-fun night!

#3 Parmesan Chicken Sandwiches
(Audrey Doty)

I like to make Parmesan Chicken Sandwiches for my supper-swapping group during busy weeks when Mike has parent-teacher conferences or baseball games keeping us busy. It takes only about 15 minutes to assemble them, and I usually add a simple side like french fries or a sweet dessert like Peanut Butter Cereal Bars (see page 231). It's also a fantastic idea to keep the ingredients on hand for a quick and easy meal on your nonswapping nights.

Simply place a single layer of 6 breaded chicken patties on a coated glass baking dish. Lay 1 slice of mozzarella cheese on top of each patty, then pour about 8 ounces of spaghetti sauce on top. Bake at 350 degrees for 45 minutes or until cheese melts and chicken is hot. Serve on hamburger buns as sandwiches or with spaghetti.

MEALTIME PRAYERS FOR THE WHOLE FAMILY

Here are some of our favorite family prayers. They are all kid friendly, easy to memorize, and can be spoken or sung. Most of these prayers came into our family through attending Camp Luther, a family church camp in Conneaut, Ohio (www.lomocamps.org). I want to thank our Camp Luther family for providing me with these wonderful family prayers to share with all of you.

God Is Great
God is great, God is good.
And we thank him for our food.
Through his love we all are fed.
Give us Lord, our daily bread. Amen.

Happy Hearts
We thank you, Lord, for happy hearts,
For rain and sunny weather.
We thank you, God, for this our food,
And that we are together.
Thank you, thank you, thank you, God.

Thank you, thank you, Father.

Thank you, thank you for our food,

And that we are together. Amen.

Johnny Appleseed

Oh, the Lord is good to me, and so I thank the Lord.

For giving me the things I need, the sun and the rain and the apple seed.

The Lord is good to me. Amen.

Come and Dine

Come and dine the Master calleth, come and dine.

He is present at our table all the time.

Christ who fed the multitudes,

Changed the water into wine,

Come and dine the Master calleth, come and dine. Amen.

Be Present at Our Table Lord

Be present at our table, Lord.

Be here and everywhere adored.

These mercies bless and grant that we,

May strengthen for thy service be

Amen, amen, amen, amen, amen.

Thanks Be

Thanks be to God the Father Almighty,

Thanks be to God who came to this earth.

Thanks be to God the Spirit eternal.

Thanks be to God forever. Amen.

We Will Thank You

Heavenly Father, Lord and King,

You provide us with everything.

We've got food on our plates, tasting great,

Thanks for what we already ate,

Singing thank you, Father, thank you.

Thank you, Father, thank you. Amen.

God Is Great

God is great.

God is good,

And we thank him for our food.

We're gonna thank him in the mornin', noon, and night,

We're gonna thank our God 'cause he's out of sight.

Amen, amen, amen, amen, amen.

For additional children's prayers, camp songs, and fun ideas, check out:

www.trishberg.com

Thank You for This Day: Action Prayers, Songs, and Blessings for Every Day by Debbie Trafton O'Neal and Nancy Munger

Children's Book of Table Blessings and *Children's Book of Family Blessings* by Ellen J. Kendig and Phyllis V. Saroff

COOKING TABLES AND INFORMATION

Food Handling and Safety

Do not allow cold food to be at room temperature for more than two hours. (The standard rule by the USDA is to keep cold foods cold, below forty degrees.)

Do not allow hot foods to remain at room temperature for more than two hours. (The standard rule by the USDA is to keep hot foods hot, above 140 degrees.)

Never leave foods at room temperature to thaw. Thaw foods only in the refrigerator or in the microwave. Once thawed, completely cook food immediately.

When delivering your meals, never let food sit in the car for more than thirty minutes, depending on the outside temperature. Deliver meals promptly, and place in fridge or oven immediately upon delivery.

For questions on food handling and safety, contact your local health department; your extension home economics department; or the USDA's meat and poultry hotline, 800-535-4555, available weekdays 10:00 a.m.–4:00 p.m. EST.

Or, call the Centers for Disease Control and Prevention Foodborne Illness Line at 404-332-4597 with twenty-four-hour recorded information available.

Equivalent Measures

3 teaspoons	= 1 tablespoon
4 tablespoons	= 1/4 cup
5 tablespoons + 1 teaspoon	= 1/3 cup
8 tablespoons	= 1/2 cup
12 tablespoons	= 3/4 cup
16 tablespoons	= 1 cup (8 ounces)
2 cups	= 1 pint (16 ounces)
4 cups (2 pints)	= 1 quart (32 ounces)
8 cups (4 pints)	= 1/2 gallon (64 ounces)
4 quarts	= 1 gallon (128 ounces)

Food	If your recipe calls for ...	You will need approximately ...
Apples	1 c. sliced or chopped	1 medium apple (6 oz)
Bacon	1/2 c. crumbled	8 slices, crisply cooked
Broccoli	2 c. chopped	6 oz.
Carrots	1 c. diced	2 medium carrots
Cauliflower	3 c. flowerets	1 lb.
Cheese, shredded	1 c. shredded	4 oz.
Cream cheese	1 c.	8 oz.
Chocolate chips	1 c.	4 oz.
Cream, sour	1 c.	8 oz.
Eggs	1 c.	4 large eggs
Egg whites	1 c.	7 to 8 large eggs
Flour	3 1/2 c.	1 lb.
Garlic	1/2 t.	1 medium clove
Lettuce	1 medium head	1 1/2 lbs.
Margarine or butter	2 c.	1 lb.
Marshmallows	1 large	10 miniature
Meat, cooked (beef, poultry, or pork)	1 c. diced	6 oz.
Mushrooms	6 c. sliced	1 lb.
Nuts	1 c.	4 oz.
Onions	1/2 c. chopped	1 medium onion
Pasta, macaroni, egg noodles, spaghetti	4 c. cooked	6-8 oz. uncooked, dry
Peppers	1/2 c. chopped	1 small pepper
Potatoes, new	10 to 12 small	1 1/2 lbs.
Potatoes, baking	1 c.	1 medium potato
Rice	3 c. cooked	1 c. uncooked
Strawberries	4 c. sliced	1 qt. strawberries
Tomatoes	1 c. chopped	1 large tomato

ALL THE SUPPER-SWAPPING RESOURCES YOU WILL NEED

The Supper-Swap-Mom Web site, www.trishberg.com

- Download free printable meal calendars to make your meal-planning gatherings go smoothly.
- Get great supper-swapping recipes free!
- Sign up for a free weekly tip from Trish on *Simplifying Motherhood*.
- Great links to all your online supper-swapping resources.
- Contact Trish if you have any other questions; share your own supper-swapping story; or just say hi.

Books on Meal Simplification

- *Once-a-Month Cooking: A Proven System for Spending Less Time in the Kitchen and Enjoying Delicious, Homemade Meals Everyday* by Mary Beth Lagerborg and Mimi Wilson
- *Supper Swapping: Cook Four Days a Month with Chefs' and Restaurants' Easy Recipes* by Susan Thacker (www.supperswapping.com)
- *Cooking Among Friends: Meal Planning and Preparation Delightfully Simplified* by Mary Tennant and Becki Visser (www.cookingamongfriends.com)
- *Frozen Assets: How to Cook for a Day and Eat for a Month* by Deborah Taylor-Hough

Recipe Resources

- *Beyond Macaroni and Cheese* by Mary Beth Lagerborg and Karen J. Parks
- The Food Network (www.foodtv.com)
- Cooking.com (www.cooking.com/recipes)
- Recipes.com (www.recipes.com)
- Club Mom (www.mom.com/go/cooking)
- *Simple & Delicious* (www.bestsimplerecipes.com)

Supper Swapping—Retail Methods

- Dream Dinners (www.dreamdinners.com)
- Dinner by Design (www.dinnerbydesignkitchen.com)

Bibliography

Adams, Nate. *The Home Team: Spiritual Practices for a Winning Family.* Grand Rapids: Revell, 2004.

The American Cancer Society. "Fruits and Vegetables: Do You Get Enough? Prevention and Early Detection." http://www.cancer.org (accessed February 25, 2006).

Betty Crocker's New Cookbook: Everything You Need to Know to Cook. New York: Macmillan, 1996.

Bliss, Rosalie Marion. "Survey Links Fast Food, Poor Nutrition Among U.S. Children." USDA Agricultural Research Service. http://www.ars.usda.gov/is/pr/2004/040105.htm (accessed February 25, 2006).

Chatzky, Jean. "Stop Getting Eaten Alive by Grocery Bills." *Money,* January 2006, 34–35.

Copeland, Mark A. "Executable Outlines, 1992–2005." Christian Classics Ethereal Library. http://www.ccel.org/contrib/exec_outlines/re/re_02.htm (accessed February 25, 2006).

DeBroff, Stacy. "The Erosion of the Family Dinner." *Mom Central.* http://www.momcentral.com/index.php?option=com_content&task=view&id=222&Itemid=3 (accessed February 25, 2006).

Dess, Nancy K. "Tend and Befriend." *Psychology Today,* September 1, 2000. http://www.psychologytoday.com/articles/pto-20000901-000021.html (accessed February 28, 2006).

"Food Groups to Encourage." USDA Dietary Guidelines for Americans. 2005. http://www.health.gov/dietaryguidelines/dga2005/recommendations.htm (accessed December 29, 2006).

The Interactive Bible. www.bible.ca/evangelism/e-inviting.htm (accessed December 28, 2006).

Leong, Pamela. "Television—A Sleeping Giant?" *Life Time.* (10:7). Ohio State University. http://www.ag.ohio-state.edu/~lifework/lifetime/vol10is7.htm (accessed July 17, 2006).

Puchalski, Christina M. "Forgiveness: Spiritual and Medical Implications." *The Yale Journal for Humanities in Medicine*, September 17, 2002. www.info.med.yale.edu (accessed February 25, 2006).

Renfroe, Anita. *The Purse-Driven Life*. Colorado Springs: NavPress, 2005.

"Ten Benefits of Frequent Family Dinners." The National Center on Addiction and Substance Abuse (CASA). Columbia University. (September 13, 2005). www.casacolumbia.org/absolutenm/templates/PressReleases.asp ?articleid=404&zoneid=64 (accessed February 25, 2006).

Vaux, Bert. "The Dialect Survey." 2000–2005. Harvard University. http://cfprod01.imt.uwm.edu/Dept/FLL/linguistics/dialect/staticmap s /q_96.html (accessed February 26, 2006).

Wang, Shirley. "Contagious Behavior." *The Observer* (19:2, 2006) http://www.psychologicalscience.org/observer/getArticle.cfm?id=193 1 (accessed February 25, 2006).

Weinstein, Miriam. *The Surprising Power of Family Meals: How Eating Together Makes Us Smarter, Stronger, Healthier, and Happier*. Hanover, NH: Steerforth Press, 2005.

Women and Friendship. The Dawn. http://www.liveandlearn.com.au/Dawn/52/friendship52.html (accessed February 25, 2006).

About the Author

Trish Berg and her husband, Mike, live with their four children on a beef-cattle farm in the heart of Ohio. For the past thirteen years, Trish has been a part-time college professor at Wayne College and a full-time mom at home. Trish's ministry is helping moms simplify the small stuff so they can get back to the joy of motherhood. She is a columnist for *The Daily Record* and has written more than one hundred articles in national and regional publications, including *MOMSense*, *P31 WOMAN*, CBN.com, and *Today's Christian Woman*.

Recipe Index

Main Dishes

Side Dishes

Talk with Trish about Supper Swapping!

If you are thinking of forming your own supper-swapping group or are already swapping and would like me to call your group for free, contact me through my Web site, www.trishberg.com.

We can set up a date and time for me to "visit" with your group via a fifteen-minute phone call. (No charge, of course!) I'll answer all of your supper-swapping questions, offer your group advice and encouragement, and I'll have the added blessing of getting to know you and all your friends!

Don't forget to visit www.trishberg.com to print out free supper-swapping calendars and meal-instruction sheets as well as other downloadables to help you simplify motherhood.

I look forward to hearing from you soon!

Blessings,
Trish Berg

My Supper-Swapping Recipes!

Add Your Supper-Swapping Recipes to

Share with Others

Recipe

Provided by

Recipe

Provided by

Recipe

Provided by

_____

_____

_____

_____

_____

_____

_____

_____

_____

_____

_____

_____

_____

_____

_____

_____

_____

_____

_____

_____

_____

_____

_____

_____

_____

_____

_____

_____

_____

_____

_____

Recipe

Provided by

Recipe

Provided by

_____

_____

_____

_____

_____

_____

_____

_____

_____

_____

_____

_____

_____

_____

_____

_____

_____

_____

_____

_____

_____

_____

_____

_____

_____

_____

_____

_____

_____

_____

_____

_____

_____

Additional copies of *The Great American Supper Swap*
are available wherever good books are sold.

If you have enjoyed this book, or if it has had an impact on your life,
we would like to hear from you.

Please contact us at

Life Journey
Cook Communications Ministries, Dept. 201
4050 Lee Vance View
Colorado Springs, CO 80918

Or visit our Web site
www.cookministries.com